Nigeria:
Actual Problems, Practical Solutions.

OSIRIAME OBALABI EDEIPO

NIGERIA: ACTUAL PROBLEMS, PRACTICAL SOLUTIONS.
© OSIRIAME O. EDEIPO 2022

Published by:
OASIS OF GREATNESS PUBLISHERS LTD.
Benin City, Edo State
Email: oasisofgreatness@gmail.com.
Website: www.oasispublishers.com
Tel.: +2348095908522, +2348082030000

ISBN: 9798848233285

<u>Also by Osiriame O. Edeipo</u>
1. Making them the Joseph of their Generation
2. How I wish
3. Osiriame… the gift of a Child
4. How to make Millions on Campus and yet be an Academic Genius
5. Our Youth have gone Mad and other stories
6. Academic and Career Success Guide (co-authored)
7. To Serve Nigeria is not by Force

<u>Watch out for the following books by Osiriame O. Edeipo</u>
1. I pledge to Nigeria my Country
2. Cure for Madness

Table of Contents

Dedication

To all Nigerians that are qualified to be counted among the "good".

Foreword

Nigeria is a typical example of an irony. A nation massively blessed with natural and human resources, yet tops the charts in all the negatives. What baffles every sensible mind is the fact that, everyday in this country, things seem only to move from bad to worse and there is no respite in sight. Reason? The vested sinister interest of a few makes the narrative continuously ugly. Their activities make the entire system "busy" and unnecessarily complicated. It takes a detailed mind to understand the situation and proffer solutions.

This book is therefore that untainted expository of the complicated causes of Nigeria's ugly narratives stated in plain and simple language. Osiriame is a pacesetter in churning out pragmatic solutions. A careful read of this piece will prove this point. What he calls "the five monsters" has indeed done the nation great evil and it is hoped that their grip on this great nation will soon be loosened.

The deliberate expulsion of Nigeria's best brains to greener pastures is a point he beautifully handled and we could only wish that this sad reality will be a thing of the past soon. Even the crude way Nigerian citizens who reside abroad are handled when they return home did not escape the author's pen. The Nigerian Press, the Nigerian youth, the over dependence on crude oil and refusal to buy Made-in-Nigeria goods - all got fair and detailed comments from Osiriame's pen.

I gladly want to encourage you to read every line in this book because each line, if well understood and it's lessons applied, will be a great step towards eradicating the ugly narratives. Happy reading and I hope you will join the vanguard of "good men" that this nation badly needs now.

Stay safe and resilient.

Fred Ekpe Ayokhai, Ph.D, is an Associate Professor at the Department of History and International Studies, Federal University of Lafia, Nasarawa State.

Email: ayokhainekpe@gmail.com

Prologue

THE HARMONIOUS TALK OF GOOD MEN

The world will not be destroyed by those who do evil,
but by those who watch them without doing anything
- Albert Einstein.

great man called Edward Burke, author of *Reflections on the Revolution in France* wrote these powerful words over 200 years ago[1]:

Whilst men are linked together, they easily and speedily communicate the alarm of any evil design. They are enabled to fathom it with common counsel, and to oppose it with united strength. Whereas, when they lie dispersed, without concert, order, or discipline, communication is uncertain, counsel difficult, and resistance impracticable. Where men are not acquainted with each other's principles, nor experienced in each other's talents, nor at all practised in their mutual habitudes and dispositions by joint efforts in business; no personal confidence, no friendship, no common interest, subsisting among them; it is evidently impossible that they can act a public part with uniformity, perseverance, or efficacy. In a connection, the most inconsiderable man, by adding to the weight of the whole, has his value, and his use; out of it, the greatest talents are wholly unserviceable to the public. No man, who is not inflamed by vain-glory into enthusiasm, can flatter himself that his single, unsupported, desultory, unsystematic endeavours, are of power to defeat the subtle designs and united cabals of ambitious citizens. When bad men combine, the good must associate; else they will fall, one by one, an unpitied sacrifice in a contemptible struggle.

In an abridged form, what he meant is that "The only thing necessary for the triumph of evil is for good men to do nothing". His position is the urgent strong cord we need to tie the center of our nationhood, if things must not be allowed to fall apart. If it does, It is, however, not a one man's affair. The harmonious efforts of all like-minded good men is therefore a sine qua non.

In the first volume of this series, I stated emphatically that I got the inspiration to write these books when I read Chinua Achebe's *The Trouble With Nigeria.* In that said volume, I made two fundamental statements that are important to this present work. Firstly, I took a slight detour from a famous Achebe's quote and stated that **the trouble with Nigeria is simply and squarely the failure of leadership and followership.**[2] Secondly, I also stated that **often in this country, we pursue the shadows of our problems and neglect the substance.** A fusion of these two positions shows us that it is high time we began to call a spade a spade. Who will do the talking or take bold physical steps (if need be)? They are the good men in this country that do not in any way support the evils that seems to have surreptitiously covered our entire nation. Also, in the previous volume, my attention was more on our serious lack of basic physical stuffs like electric power, good roads, food, etc. In this volume, my attention will be beamed mainly on intangible concepts that have done us a thousand and one ills. Rather than being angry, I expect those indicted to feel remorse and desist from their dastardly acts. The good men that abhor such acts must, as a matter of urgency, come out of their shells and do the needful - speak harmoniously in favour of what is right and be prepared to defend their positions by all means. Our tomorrow as a people may currently look very bleak but I do sincerely hope that this volume will further open our eyes to the root causes of the "worms" that have destroyed our "game" – (See the Prologue of my book *To Serve Nigeria Is Not By Force* for better understanding). I strongly believe that Nigeria will be truly great in no distant time if we do what is right. As said earlier on, it will however, require the selfless harmonious talks and actions of great good men. Will you be among the "good" that will join this great and noble struggle?

Osiriame Edeipo,
May, 2022.

Works cited
1. https://harpers.org/2007/11/burke-on-why-men-of-good-will-must-unite/
2. Edeipo Osiriame. To Serve Nigeria is Not By Force. Oasis of Greatness Publishers Limited, Benin City, 2021, P. 5.

Introduction:

MY DSC
EXPERIENCE

One who sees perceives. One who hears understands. One who grasps comprehends. One who believes knows - Matshona Dhliwayo.

I did my mandatory 6 Months industrial training at the Training Centre of Delta Steel Company, Ovwian-Aladja, Delta State in the Year 2000. As at then, that multi-billion-dollar project did not produce one gram of steel for more than four years prior to my arrival and staffs salaries were owed for an equivalent number of years.

Two of my classmates and I did our IT at DSC at the same time. Although we got good training in the use of Lathe, Milling, Welding, Drilling, Folding machines, as well as other related exposures, we were justly worried that it would be absurd that we did our industrial attachment in a Steel Plant and we had zero knowledge about steel production. Our worries got to the ears of a kind-hearted Senior Engineer that worked in DSC when DSC was fully functional. He then volunteered to take us on an excursion to the Main Steel Plant. The distance from the Training Centre to the Main Steel Plant should be about 800 meters to and fro and all through the trip, he gave us both engineering and non-engineering lectures. I won't bore you with the engineering lectures but I will tell you the non-engineering tales because when we saw gigantic world-class machines that the Steel complex had - all covered with thick layer of dust and cobwebs, his talk stuck firmly to our brains. No matter how advanced a machine is, if the man or men handling it are crude, careless or greedy, the machine cannot do much. The following are some of the disturbing tales he told us about what led to the down fall of DSC:

1. He said when DSC was to be built, the initial architectural design of the Admin Block were simple, cost effective set of storey buildings. Pride made the decision makers to throw away the design and they went for a gigantic edifice that had elevators and all manner of modern gadgets that made the final building; several time costlier than the initial design. As at the time we did our IT, that gigantic Admin Bock looked like an old museum because the "administrative thievery" that took place in that big building ruined the entire outfit to the sad extent of it not being able to produce one gram of steel. To what use then is a 'Big Admin Block', if the company cannot live up to its expectations?

2. When DSC began to have problem with production, the then Minister of Internal Affairs ordered that DSC must be made to pay import duty for the Electrodes she used to melt steel. The then top management of DSC went to see their immediate boss - The then Honorable Minister of Mines and Power. This incident happened during the era Nigeria was being governed by the Military. After explaining the devastating effects the new cost will have on the ailing company, the Honorable Minister was furious, calling them names. Reason? He could not understand why they were making noise about importation of electrode

"when electrodes filled everywhere!" For him, the electrode that is used in a Steel Plant is the same with the one that the roadside welder used to do his welding work. It took them a while to convince the Honorable Minister of Mines and Power that the electrode that is used to melt steel industrially is a gigantic one that is as tall as a storey building. If the Honorable Minister of Mines and Power did not have an iota of knowledge about the working mechanism of one of the most important establishments under his Ministry, then one is forced to ask, how did he get to that position in the first place and if DSC were the personal company of the person that gave him the appointment, would he appoint someone that has less than 20% knowledge of the working principles of the steel complex to head it? Now the big question that I want you to muse on is "how well does a square peg fit into a round hole?"

3. One of the Chief Executive Officers of the Steel Company was to bury one of his parents. He then "borrowed" a gigantic industrial generator that belongs to the steel complex and took it to his hometown in order to give the departed a "befitting burial". The generator left the gate of DSC but never returned till (perhaps) date. The services that the generator would have provided was terminated and I wonder what value that massive generator added to the village or villagers after the burial?

Nobody challenged the CEO when he gave the stupid idea of moving the generator to his hometown and nobody queried him when the generator's "feet" became "too heavy" to return to the complex. Where in the world is such madness tolerated?

4. Indiscriminate employment and reckless award of contract was the order of the day when DSC was DSC. Reason? No matter how much you spend from DSC coffers, Almighty DSC was too big to fall. That was the mentality then, but today, that stupid mindset has turned out to be a fallacy that is too expensive to be tolerated by a people. I see this mindset in the way people generally handle public money in Nigeria. If nothing is done to stop this madness, Nigeria may someday fall, the same way DSC fell many years back.

Before you sound religious and say "God forbid" I want you to know that progress in life generally operate on principles that God himself ordained. Violating them and expecting bliss is equivalent to telling God to His face that the rules or laws He ordained are rubbish. These aforementioned points will be cited on a regular note in the course of making many arguments stand on their feet in this book.

Chapter One

CABAL, OCCULTISM, CULTISM, AGBEROISM & GODFATHERISM

> *Neither the wisest constitution nor the wisest laws will secure the liberty and happiness of a people whose manner are universally corrupt*
> *- Samuel Adams.*

One of the most significant reasons men gather together to form societies, whether great or small, is the dire need to promote peaceful co-existence. Peaceful coexistence in a progressive setting is often achieved through adherence to the laws of the land. Before man became learned enough to write down laws in form of a constitution, laws governing every known society were clearly spelt out to all its inhabitants and adherence was expected of all. The degree of adherence is often directly proportional to the political and economic growth of the people.

Till date, the *status quo* has not changed in the sense that, a society, where the rule of law is keenly obeyed, is often a very progressive society (and vice versa). We will therefore, quickly define the term "Rule of law".

Rule of law, according to Dictionary.com is[1] *"the principle that all people and institutions are subject to and accountable to a law that is fairly applied and enforced; the principle of government by law"*. Merriam Webster Dictionary makes the meaning easier to comprehend. It says it is[2] *"a situation in which the laws of a country are obeyed by everyone"*. Yes! Everyone should truly be "everyone" when matters concerning obeying the laws of the land are raised. It was against this backdrop that the great Greek philosopher, called Aristotle said[3] *"it is more proper that law should govern than any one of the citizens"*. A situation where some "people and institutions" are not subject to or accountable to the law is indeed pitiable and highly detrimental to progress. A situation where some persons governs more than the law (in fact, they are the law) is totally unacceptable and it can be likened to heating a volatile liquid – like petrol in a Pressure Cooker. It may take a while for an explosion to take place but a discontinuance of such a nasty experiment is often the wisest things to do because the eruption from that experiment can be liken to anarchy and when anarchy sets in, virtually nobody in the land is spared from the "particles" of the eruption that follows.

In Nigeria, this nasty experiment is a reoccurring decimal that is perpetrated by several group of persons that believe they control the economy or politics of the nation. Their partial or total disregard for the law is often carried out with reckless abandon. One is then forced to ask: When did evil become good or good become evil? When did the government become a toothless bulldog that cannot bark let alone bite? Who or what, removed the blindfold that covers the eyes of the Lady of Justice and hence, she is now partial in Nigeria? If some persons that rule us today are above the law, why should they not expect others that will be in power tomorrow not to try to exceed their madness – as if such madness were a game that gives a handsome reward to the highest jumper? If ….

The list of mind-bugging questions that high-profile lawlessness that operate in Nigeria beam daily on a well cultured mind is simply outrageous. This high level of lawlessness is, sadly, a pointer to what enlightened minds call a Failed State. A Failed State is a country that can no longer exercise full authority over its people and territory and hence, it finds it difficult to protect its national borders or relate sovereignly with other nations.

Wikipedia gave four features of a failed state and they are as follows:[4]

· Loss of control of its territory, or of the monopoly on the legitimate use of physical force
· Erosion of legitimate authority to make collective decisions
· Inability to provide public services
· Inability to interact with other states as a full member of the international community

It is quite unfortunate that the first three of these features are the current realities in present day Nigeria. It is an ugly situation where some individuals freely use crude force against their countrymen and nobody (including security operatives) dare challenge them; and the decision of such men at times override the position of the government; and they therefore decide to what extent citizens can have access to public services or public facilities. If nothing drastic is done, we may soon find ourselves in the domain of the fourth feature - a situation where these men will completely decide our relationship with the international community or they deal directly with them and our legitimate government will toe behind them like secondary school students that followed a teacher to an external competition. Some decisive steps must be taken soon or ....

I will therefore, try to pursue the substance of my position by talking about some groups of men and women in Nigeria that are above the law and their ill activities. They are a set I call "The five Monsters."

CABAL

The word Cabal did not mean much in the vocabulary of many Nigerians until sometimes in 2011 when there was a great fuel scarcity all over the federation and the then President, Dr. Goodluck Ebele Jonathan, said "cabals" were responsible for the colossal mess that plunged more than 180 million people into untold hardship[5].

If the Commander-in-Chief that was completely in charge of our Armed Forces that comprises of Army, Air Force and Navy; as well as other paramilitary groups like the Nigerian Police, Customs, Immigration, Prison, etc said he was incapacitated to remedy a national crisis because of a group he calls "Cabal," then what can an ordinary citizen do to these men in high places?

Wikipedia defines cabal as a[6] *"group of people who are united in some close design, usually to promote their private views or interest in an ideology, a state, or another community, often by intrigue and usually unbeknown to those who are outside their group."* The Britannica Dictionary put it in a direct and simplified form by stating that a cabal is[7] *"a small group of people who work together secretly".* The secret agenda of this small group of persons is often inimical to the good of the majority of persons outside the group. It is quite sad to note that in virtually every aspect of our national life, a cabal exists to a small and great extent. Tomatoes seller's cabal, motor spare parts cabals, transporters cabals, civil servants cabal, lecturers cabal, bankers cabal, etc. are some few cases I can readily mention. Our attention is on the group popularly known as Oil Cabal.

Officially, oil was first discovered in Oloibiri in 1956 and from then till date, it has been the mainstay of the Nigerian economy. It is, therefore, not surprising that a group of persons all these years has made themselves demigods in the oil sector and milked the country dry through it. The manifestation of their wickedness and greed can be felt on our national purse yearly in the name of "fuel subsidy". Before I analyse the gravity of the mess these oil cabal or better still "oil thieves", have plunged this whole nation into, permit me to educate you about the origin of fuel subsidy in Nigeria.

A veteran of the Nigeria Oil and Gas sector that wishes to be anonymous told me that he did his NYSC programme at Port Harcourt Refinery when the entire complex performed excellently. Nigerian Engineers, led by one Engr. Okoli, handled the day to day running of the refinery and they did so perfectly for many years. He said the old refinery was built before Nigeria Civil War and it had the capacity to produce 60,000 barrels per day. It worked for 11 months and it was then shut down for a month's routine maintenance. Prior to the one month maintenance, excess production was made and stored in tank farms but it was never enough to satisfy our teeming local consumption. That was what gave rise to giving license to some individual by the government to import petrol. To meet our rising population, the then Nigerian Government built a new refinery by a Japanese Company called Chiyoda, and it had the capacity to produce 150,000 barrels per day. When the new refinery was finally commissioned, there was no need to give anybody license that year and it did not go well with those that were used to getting it. These greedy men that we now call Oil Cabal, then made arrangement with one of the members of staff of the refinery to deliberately put fire on one of the refineries – an act that then forced the government to resume issuing license to individuals to import petroleum product. From that time on, both refineries began to deteriorate because of (deliberate) bad management.

When he finally visited the refineries ten years after his service year, he could not believe his eyes at the rapid deterioration both refineries had "enjoyed." For this veteran of the oil industry, these oil cabals are the ones that makes it difficult for us to have functional government owned refineries in Nigeria because they always put their personal economic interest first, before national interest.

From the above information, it is clear that these "big thieves" in high places have never meant well for this country and they will never want a stop to this most inhumane treatment they dole out to the Nigerian nation as a whole. For me, their crime against the Nigerian people is worse when compared to that of our Colonial Masters. Reason? Our Colonial Master took raw materials like cocoa, coffee and tobacco from Nigeria to Europe and used their machines and technical know-how (which we did not have as at then) to transform the raw products into finished goods and shipped them back to us and we had no choice than to buy them at whatever price they gave us.

On the other hand, these oil cabals lift crude oil from Nigeria, pay to transport it to other countries, pay to have it refined over there and in the process, create massive employment /great revenue for that country and pay another cut throat amount to transport the finished product back to Nigeria. The landing cost of course would be high but the Nigerian government will then pay them handsomely for, permit me to say, "such irresponsibility". Why do I call it irresponsibility? Permit me to post a powerful article from *Business Day online Newspaper* written by Oladehinde Oladipo on March 5, 2022.[8]

> Buoyed by the rise in global crude oil prices, the subsidy being incurred on petrol by the Nigerian government has risen to an estimated N10 billion daily, a *Business Day* analysis of industry data has shown.
>
> The landing cost of petrol imported into the country was N309.87 per litre on February 25, using the official exchange rate of N416.46/$.
>
> With daily petrol consumption put at about 60 million litres by the Nigerian National Petroleum Company and a subsidy of N168.87 per litre, the daily subsidy amounts to N10.1 billion as the pump price of the product remains steady at N162-N165 per litre.
>
> "With rising oil prices, Nigeria's current petrol subsidy is very enormous and is hitting Nigeria's crude income very deeply," Mike Osatuyi, national operations controller of the Independent Petroleum Marketers Association Nigeria (IPMAN), told *Business Day*. The international oil benchmark, Brent crude, the gauge for Nigeria's crude, jumped to $118 per barrel on Friday

from $77.24 per barrel on December 31, 2021. "The current market reality shows Nigeria pays about N17 billion daily on petrol subsidy," Osatuyi said.

Cheta Nwanze, a partner at SBM Intelligence, an Africa-focused geopolitical firm, predicts Nigeria's 2022 subsidy spend would be the highest on record, surpassing the former administration's records. "Nigeria is in a deeper financial hole than it has ever been, and the only thing the government has done is to dig even deeper," he said.

An analysis of data collated by *Business Day* showed that without subsidy, petrol would be selling for about N333.099 per litre as of February 25. Further analysis of the petroleum pricing template showed the cost of petrol quoted on Platts stood at $918.75 per metric tonne (N285.33 per litre, using the I&E rate of N416.33/$1) on February 25 2022 from $754.75 per MT on December 31, 2021, with a freight cost of $26.77 per MT (N8.31 per litre). Other cost elements that make up the landing cost include lightering expenses (N4.81), Nigerian Ports Authority charge (N2.49), Nigerian Maritime Administration and Safety Agency charge (N0.23), jetty throughput charge (N1.61), storage charge (N2.58), and financing (N2.17).

The pump price is the sum of the landing cost, wholesaler margin (N4.03), admin charge (N1.23), transporters allowance (N3.89), bridging fund (N7.51), marine transport average (N0.15), and retailer margin (N6.19).

"Before the end of 2022, Nigeria's petrol subsidy will hit N6 trillion," Kelvin Atafiri, who runs Cavazzani Human Capital Limited, an investment firm exposed to the oil and gas sector, said. The NNPC said, recently, that it spent N210.38 billion on petrol subsidy in January 2022. According to NNPC's latest presentation at Federation Accounts Allocation Committee (FAAC) meeting, the shortfall included a December 2021 value of PMS shortfall of N176.48 billion plus the outstanding value shortfall recovery of N33.90 billion accrued over 2021. The oil firm said it would deduct N242.5 billion (about N143.7 billion for January 2022 recovery and November spot arrears of N98.8 billion) during next month's FAAC meeting. Further checks showed that NNPC did not remit any money to the FAAC for onward distribution to the federating units. Findings by Business Day showed FAAC allocation declined by 17 percent to N574.668 billion in January 2022. "Subsidy payment is a gorilla that has swallowed

Nigeria's economy and has led to the collapse of education institutions, road infrastructures and health facilities," said Wumi Iledare, a professor of economics and former president of Nigerian Association for Energy Economics

Let's analyze this article together:

1. We are told the FG spend ₦10,000,000,000 daily on fuel subsidy and in a year that will amount to ₦10,000,000,000 x 365 = ₦3,650,000,000,000.

That is a whopping 3.65 trillion naira!

If we are to invest this money into building refineries what can it do for us?

There are basically two types of refineries

i. Modular refineries and ii. Conventional refinery.

Modular Refineries are often smaller than the Conventional Refineries and of course, they are cheaper. Although, they may not be able to break down crude oil into smaller or finer products like the conventional refineries but they can convert crude oil into kerosene and diesel. When crackers are installed in these small refineries, they can produce petrol. Why can't we set up modular refineries and install crackers that will make them produce petrol for us? Go online and you will see the numerous bottlenecks that cabals, speaking through the mouth of NNPC have set up to frustrate such moves.

The last time I checked, a modular refinery that can produce 100,000 barrels per day cost 1.5 Billion Dollars and the one that can produce 24,000 barrels per day cost 250 Million Dollars. How many of such refineries can 3.65 Trillion Naira that we "dash" the Cabals virtually every year gives us? At the official rate of ₦415.48 - approximately ₦416, we have

250,000 x 416 = ₦104,000,000,000

1,500,000,000 x 416 = ₦624,000,000,000

Dividing ₦3.65trillion by the first figure, will give 35.096 – approximately 35

Divide ₦3.65 trillion by the second figure, will give 5.849 – approximately 6

What does this figure tells you and me? With the money we spend on subsidy for a year we can build a 24,000 barrel-per-day modular refinery in 35 oil fields and we will have no need to risk our crude oil being stolen by pipeline vandals or we can use same money to build 100,000 barrel-per-day modular refinery in 6 viable fields. But let's do the some further calculations together:

36 x 24000 = 864,000

6 x 100,000 = 600,000

If we take our mind back to the DSC Admin Block story I narrated in my introductory notes, we can clearly see that to purchase the smaller modular refineries will give us more returns for the same amount of money. Did you know that such modular refineries will produce more petroleum products for us than Dangote's yet to be completed refinery that has a daily capacity of 650,000 barrels per day? Moreover, such moves will create more jobs and bring the market closer to the people. Yet, some self-centered individual will cite "environmental factors" as a bane to such moves or out rightly resist the building of any of the two refineries (as they have done for many years).

Although, the figures quoted above is a far cry from what NNPC claim we consume in a day, but remember that Rome was not built in a day and a journey of a thousand miles often start with a step. To build 35 more modular refinery in a country that Cabals have milked dry in the name of fuel subsidy is not just a step but a giant step. How about using that money to completely refurbish all government owned refineries and sacking all the current top brass that are there and don't know what to do? If we then go into partnership with the private sector that will make sure that we stop hearing the appalling stories of a thousand and one reasons government refineries can't work, don't you think we will score a huge point in economic recovery and the crazy figures we waste on subsidy will be used to build other sectors in Nigeria that are begging for help?

2.   "Further analysis of the petroleum pricing template showed the cost of petrol quoted on Platts stood at $918.75 per metric

tonne (N285.33 per litre, using the I&E rate of N416.33/$1) on February 25 2022 from $754.75 per MT on December 31, 2021, with a freight cost of $26.77 per MT (N8.31 per litre). Other cost elements that make up the landing cost include lightering expenses (N4.81), Nigerian Ports Authority charge (N2.49), Nigerian Maritime Administration and Safety Agency charge (N0.23), jetty throughput charge (N1.61), storage charge (N2.58), and financing (N2.17)."

This statement shows the numerous persons that benefit massively from this subsidy era. Those that have ships that freight crude to and fro will never want this "lucrative businesses" to stop. Those that have tank farms too will massively do anything to ensure this madness is not cured. The various banks that provide finance and the numerous staffs of government agencies that benefit directly or indirectly from this brutalization of Nigeria in the name of fuel subsidy will equally not want it to stop. The "baddest" of them all are the "main men" themselves that have license to deal in refining crude oil. They get crazy money from the whole transaction and, definitely, they will never want it to stop. If all of them were fair in their dealings, the crime against the Nigeria people would have been milder. Some do terrible things that may not be obtainable in any other country of the world and that leads me to the third point.

3. "Subsidy payment is a gorilla that has swallowed Nigeria's

economy and has led to the collapse of education institutions, road infrastructures and health facilities," said Wumi Iledare, a professor of economics and former president of Nigerian Association for Energy Economics.

To appreciate the viewpoints of this erudite scholar, let us hear the collaborating statements of Honorable Minister of Petroleum Resources, Chief Timipre Sylvia in the post below.[10]

> Timipre Sylva, the minister of petroleum resources, says Nigeria needs to move away from the petrol subsidy regime to end its 'opaqueness'. Sylva added that Nigeria's daily petrol consumption figures are 'crazy'. And sometimes, the figures you hear are crazy. I mean, when they tell you 90 million litres a day, I mean, they're crazy figures. So I mean, so for me, what is the total of all this? We've been interrogating these numbers for 20 years. "We continue to interrogate these figures because we all know that there is a problem here, it's opaque. "The opportunity, the premium is not coming to government and it is not going to the poor people. It is going to a select people who are feeding fat on these things. "So why don't we just get rid of this thing? Okay, we should interrogate this thing, but I mean, to me, that is not the solution. Why don't we just get rid of this whole subsidy so that we know that this problem is over

once and for all? "I mean, we agree that the figures are all opaque. We agree. That's why we are saying look, let's stop all the shenanigans.

Let's stop all this discussion. "Let's leave all this opaqueness, all this corruption in the subsidy, let us move away from subsidy and go on higher ground. And then they say no. "There's been trials of subsidy thieves. We've gone on television to say okay, these are the templates, these are the components of the templates." The minister said the labour union, which is against the removal of the subsidy, knows the issues, adding that Nigeria continues to haemorrhage because the subsidy regime persists. "Why don't we just get out of it? Okay, there has been some corruption. So we can always deal with the corruption issues," Sylva said. "We can always deal with all the opaque issues. But should we allow Nigerians who are not benefiting from this thing, as you agree with me, to continue to be haemorrhaging?

"Because we need to get out of this, because look at it, N3 trillion budget. You can imagine if this N3 trillion were to be budgeted for something else. Who's going to benefit from it? I'm not into the downstream, I'm not going to benefit."

What Chief Timipre Sylvia is saying in plain terms is that some of these "Cabal" will go to NNPC and CBN and they will state that they have imported say, 2,500,000 litres of petrol but in the real sense, they imported zero litre. From the previous Business Day article, remember that the landing cost of petrol is 309.87 and Federal government make Nigerians to buy it at between ₦162 and ₦165 per litre, meaning subsidy is between 147.87 and 144.87. So a man that claimed he imported 2,500,000 litres whereas he imported zero litre, will be paid a minimum of

2,500,000 x 144.87 = ₦362,175,000

That means a whopping 362 Million Naira of public funds will land into the individual's account for doing absolutely nothing! Where in the world is such madness perpetrated by a group of persons unchecked? This hyper greed and wickedness must stop because I am certain that there is hardly any Federal or State University in Nigeria that get that much as monthly allocation for all its expenses - I stand to be corrected. Do I have evidence for my claims? Absolutely Yes. Dr, Ngozi Okonjo-Iweala wrote a book she titled *Fighting Corruption Is Dangerous* and she penned down the following:

> The committee held hearings over three months with oil marketers, the private sector, government officials, and all concerned with the oil-subsidy regime. In April 2012, it issues it's findings, including sixty-one recommendations. Essentially, the Committee found

that there was indeed fraud and mismanagement in the oil-subsidy regime; subsidy claims for products not delivered; overcharging of the government by oil marketers; requisition of foreign exchange for import of refined products, with the foreign exchange diverted to other uses; unauthorised deductions by the Nigerian National Petroleum Corporation (NNPC) to itself; and mismanagement by government officials. According to the report of the Ad-Hoc Committee:

We found that the subsidy regime as operated between the period under review (2009-2011) was fraught with endemic corruption and entrenched inefficiency. Much of the amount claimed to have been paid as subsidy was actually not for consumed PMS [petrol]. Government officials made nonsense of the (PSF) Petroleum Subsidy Fund) guidelines due mainly to sleaze and, in some cases, incompetence.It is therefore apparent that the insistence by top government official that the subsidy figures were for the products consume was a clear attempt to mislead the Nigeria people. The report made several important recommendations: the sum of N1.067 trillion ($6.8 billion) deemed to have been misappropriated as subsidy payments during the period under review should be repaid to the Treasury by the

Nigerian National Petroleum Corporation (NNPC), the Petroleum Products Pricing Regulatory Agency (PPPRA) and oil marketers; government agencies and officials deemed to have participated in the misappropriation or mismanagement of the subsidy regime should be sanctioned; oil marketers involved should be further investigated and prosecuted; NNPC and the Ministry of Petroleum Resources should be restructured to make their operations more transparent; and the kerosene subsidy should be continued, given its impact on poor people. The report went further to make recommendations on the amount of petroleum products the country should consume daily, how much should be budgeted for these, and a revised monitoring process for implementing the subsidy regime effectively ....

Many of these findings mirrored the findings of the House of representative Ad-Hoc Committee to Verify and Determine the Actual Subsidy Requirements, but this time the findings were meticulously researched and well-documented. The Presidential Committee found subsidy claims for shipments by "ghost vessels" that never supplied any product and for shipments by vessels that were in China and the South Pacific at the times it was claimed they were transshipping off the coast of

Cotonou, Benin. They were verified by Lloyd's Register, which track the movement of ships all over the world. They were subsidy claims for which there were no shipping document or evidence of payment for the products in foreign exchange.

Various other overpayments, wrongful claims, and breaches of the Petroleum Subsidy Fund guidelines also were detected. The Presidential Committee found that of the N1.3 trillion ($8.4 billion) verified, N382 billion ($2.5 billion) was fraudulent or questionable and should be recovered from the 107 oil marketing companies whose activities were verified. The door was left open on some questionable transactions for companies that could produce further verifiable documentations to come forward for the transaction to be validated. The report recommended that several procedural and regulatory improvement be implemented to the process for managing the subsidy. It also recommended sanctioning offending agencies and individuals, including the executive secretaries of the main regulatory agency overseeing the Petroleum Subsidy Fund, the Petroleum Products Pricing Regulatory Agency, and the external auditors of the Finance Ministry, Akintola Williams Deloitte, and Olusola Adekonola and Associates, which were found negligent in their duties.

"The Presidential Committee found that of the N1.3 trillion ($8.4 billion) verified, N382 billion ($2.5 billion) was fraudulent or questionable and should be recovered from the 107 oil marketing companies whose activities were verified." please note that the Presidential Committee recommended disciplinary action for a whooping 107 Oil Marketing Companies that were indicted and they were asked to refund the monies that they wrongly took from the State purse. Will it surprise you that the possibilities are high that till date, neither of the committee's recommendation has been carried out? The recommendations were all swept under the carpet and life goes on - the culprits smiling and rejoicing while the masses, cry and lament daily.

Another sickening problem created by Oil Cabals is oil theft. Did you know that as it stands right now, the major International Oil Companies (IOCS) in Nigeria - Shell, Chevron and Mobil are all about to completely leave Nigeria, a plan that began about 15 years ago? Reason? Let us read the comments of some of the great players in the oil and gas sector of Nigeria – I mean Mr. Austin Avuru and Mr. Tony Elumelu. Their comments can be found in an article written by Emmanuel Addeh of THISDAY Newspaper titled "Avuru Calls For State Of Emergency In Oil Sector, Says

80% Of Crude Stolen"[12]

A Co-founder and former Chief Executive Officer of Seplat Energy Plc, Mr. Austin Avuru has called for a state of emergency in the Nigerian oil and gas sector, revealing that up to 80 per cent of oil pumped in the country, particularly in the East, is stolen.

Avuru's comments came few days after a businessman and Chairman Heirs Holdings, Mr. Tony Elumelu, also bemoaned the worsening state of the industry, stressing that about 95 per cent of oil production does not get to the terminal. Elumelu has his oil assets in the Niger Delta. Elumelu also chairs the Board of the United Bank for Africa (UBA), holds a controlling interest in Transnational Corporation (Transcorp) and runs Trans-Niger Oil & Gas Limited (TNOG). The owner of TNOG, which recently bought 45 per cent of Oil Mining Licence (OML) 17, argued that oil theft was generally responsible for Nigeria's inability to meet its Organisation of Petroleum Exporting Countries (OPEC) quota.

"How can we be losing over 95 per cent of oil production to thieves? Look at the Bonny Terminal that should be receiving over 200,000bpd barrels of crude oil daily, instead it receives less than 3,000 barrels, leading the operator, Shell to declare *force majeure*," he had lamented.

But writing for Africa Oil & Gas Report, Avuru, who is the Founder/ Executive Chairman, AA Holdings and Vice Chairman Platform Petroleum, maintained that as far as 1990, Nigeria's average daily oil production was about 1.85 million barrels per day when the country's oil reserves at the time stood at about 16 billion barrels. However, he deplored the current situation in which Nigeria cannot meet the quota allocated by OPEC and had been struggling to produce 1.4 million barrels per day. He argued that aside theft of Nigeria's oil, with eyes fixed on divestments and exit, the International Oil Companies (IOCs) have not made any meaningful investments in the sector in the last 15 years, with the result being the current declining production.

"Much worse, the entire export pipeline network has been surrendered to vandals and illegal 'bunkerers'. Thus, the phrase 'crude theft' which crept into the industry about 2010 has taken on a new meaning. "There are some pipeline systems now (particularly in the East) where 80 per cent of production injected therein does not make it to the terminal! Almost every producer is now cooking up alternative evacuation schemes that cost four to five times what pipeline export would normally cost," he lamented. Avuru noted that while the decision to leave by the IOCs was outside Nigeria's control, the country's delay in passing the Petroleum Industry Bill (PIB) ensured that investment in the sector dried up a long time ago.

"In fact, my projection is that, by Christmas day of 2025, Total would be the only IOC in Joint Venture (JV) with the NNPC," he said. He pointed out that the situation was not different with domestic gas delivery, adding that even though Nigeria continues to weave all the right slogans about the future of gas in Nigeria, in the past five years, he could only point at a couple of Nigerian independents who are investing in gas development and processing for the domestic market.

"The state of the Nigerian petroleum industry is a national emergency. Oil production is down to about 1.4 million barrels per day and declining and this includes about 600,000BOPD from the deep water. "Domestic gas production has stagnated at about 1.2 billion cubic feet (Bcf) per day over the past five years at a time when projected production should have been 3.5Bcf per day. The collateral impact of course, is the low level of power generation which itself has stagnated at about 4,000 megawatts per day since 2015," the businessman said.

On recommendations, Avuru stressed that between the upstream regulator (the commission) and the Nigerian National Petroleum Company (NNPC), they need to set up a, "war room", or some form of an effective task force to develop a blueprint for returning the industry to full bloom.

"The responses we hear today to the myriad of problems outlined above have been ad-hoc, knee jerk and in some cases only self-serving. I dare repeat that the situation has to be treated as a national emergency," he explained.

He argued that a well-organised transition driven policy direction, from the retreating IOCs' needs to be developed, noting that intervening by pre-emptive acquisitions cannot be a sustainable solution proffered by the NNPC."There has to be a deliberate policy-driven return to the traditional onshore/shallow water terrains. Eighty per cent of our remaining reserves are still in this belt.

"To do this, we have to address the twin problems of reliable pipeline evacuation and community restiveness. These problems have become heightened, not because there is no solution, but because we have abandoned every attention to them in the last 15 years. "When these two problems are tackled, plus a strict application of the 'drill or drop' provisions of the new PIA, huge investments in drilling and facilities revamp will flow again into this terrain.

"Finally, we have to match our gas slogans with effective, measurable, policy actions to drive investments in domestic gas supply. The current flip-flops on pricing and commercial structure of the gas business cannot stimulate investments in the sector. "This industry will not wake up by God's miracle. We have to wake up and design the stimulant that will revitalise it," Avuru said. ...

As usual, let us analyse this article together:

1. If between 80 to 95% of oil that is produce is stolen by vandals (that have of course metamorphosed into powerful Cabals) and we have security agents in this country that have not been able to bring the criminals to book, will it not be right to say that the security men themselves and some "invisible *ogas* of the top" have a hand in this colossal evil against the Nigerian people? This evil trade has prospered *ad infinitum* because no serious punishment has been mated to those caught, if ever anybody was. If someone is caught and "settles", he is left off the hook. Such a person will of course, go back in the evil business this time with

greater caution that will plunge the nation into greater mess. So, I SERIOUSLY BLAME ALL THE COLLABORATORS in this devastating crime against Nigerians

2.   If all the major IOCs leave Nigeria because of our gross inability to protect their investment in our shores, how easy will we find it to encourage other foreign and local investors to invest their dime into our country? If Mr. Tony Elumelu (the astute Nigerian business man) got his finger burnt because of his investment in Nigeria, how do you expect him to talk to others to do same or how will any sensible foreigners see such terrible handwriting on the wall and come to invest in our shores?

3.   Avuru recommends a "war room" approach if this mad evil must be stop and I am forced to quickly ask, how long will it take to set up such a redeeming strategy? Must 100% of what is produced be stolen before the government of the day wake up to its responsibilities? Remember once upon a time, 100% of what was produced got to it terminal point. If when we noticed that as much as 10% was missing, this "war room" approach was immediately set up, we will definitely not be where we are today.

4. *The News Echo* Newspaper has this disturbing headline in one of its editions "Deadly Monsters in Nigeria's oil kingdoms." Permit me to post a portion of that write up that will give us a picture of the trouble we currently find ourselves in the oil sector:[13]

In 2021, Nigeria lost at least 3.5 billion dollars revenue to crude oil theft, a figure that represents 10% of Nigeria's foreign reserve. Oil theft and pipeline vandalism threaten oil exploration and accruable revenue. In 2019, the Nigerian National Petroleum Corporation (NNPC) announced that it lost 159 billion to oil theft and pipeline vandalization. The losses were put at 2.8 billion dollars in 2018. Although resources were appropriated for the security of oil facilities, the activities of all teams continued unabated.

With these organised oil criminal gangs making off with millions in stolen crude, Nigeria suspected to be Africa's richest economy faces its worst oil crisis in years while these oil thieves are taking in "petrodollars" on high seas while FAAC flounders.

For a century like Nigeria whose oil industry generates about two-thirds of its revenue, oil theft is no small matter.

Nigerian Navy recently announced, it has seized above 6 million litres of petroleum product worth over N3 billion from oil thieves since it launched Operation Dakatar Da Barawo (OPDDB), also known as 'Stop the Thief'....

On April 15 2022, Nigerian Navy Ship DELTA at Warri deactivated an illegal refinery sites around Sara creek, the statement reads

"The IRS has 16 ovens, 16 metal storage tanks and three wide pits filled with about 50000 litres of illegal refined AGO as well as 700000 litres of stolen crude oil, a generator and for pumping machines. Also, an IRS at Asugbo creek in Warri was discovered with six ovens, 12 metal storage tanks and five large pits all containing about 600,000 liters of stolen crude oil including 200,000 litres of illegally refined AGO and about 150,000 litres of sludge.

Similarly, sequel to series of air reconnaissance, Forward Operating Base FORMOSO in Bayelsa State on April 19, 2022 raided an IRS at Ereweibio creeks on Brass LGA. Accordingly seven large cooking ovens, 10 large metal storage tanks and drums all laden with about 400,000 of illegal refined AGO and 20,000 litres of suspected illegal refined PMS were discovered. The site also had five large pits holding approximately 700,000 litres of stolen crude oil. Equally, two pumping machines, one gasoline generator, one submersible pump and one chainsaw machine were discovered at the site and destroyed in sites.

The statement added that an IRS at Lelemu creek in Warri South West was discovered on April 21 2022. "During the operation, 19 ovens, 26 storage tanks and two dugout pit laden with over 250,000 tons of suspected stolen crude oil and 50,000 litres of illegally refined Automotive Gas Oil (AGO) were destroyed" it said.

"To ensure effectiveness deactivation of IRS, NNS Delta on 21 April 2022 conducted swamp buggy operations during which an earlier identified IRS around Egwa creek in Warri was destroyed. During the operation, 16 ovens, 31 metal storage tanks and seven large pits all filled with about 850,000 litres of stole crude oil were equally deactivated

Relatedly, on April 22, 2022, around Lelemu creek in Warri South West Local Government Area (LGA) of Delta state, personnel under NNS Delta again discover 22 IRS ovens, 12 metal storage tanks and five large pits all containing about 150,000 litres of stolen crude oil.

"At another IRS at Lelemu creek, 19 ovens, 42 storage tanks and 14 large pits containing about 300,000 litres of stolen crude oil as well as approximately 200,000 litres of illegal refined DPK and 100,000 litres of suspected crude oil sludge were all destroyed," it said.

It also noted that combing the area of Jones creek led to the discovery of another IRS with five ovens, two metal storage tanks and eight large pits with about 150,000 litres of sludge.

It said both IRS of Jones Creek with the discover items and product were destroyed in situ.

…. Reacting to the incident President Muhammadu Buhari ordered that all the sponsors of the illegal refinery should be brought to book.

The Nigeria Navy has tried but I am convinced that they need to try harder. The President has ordered the arrest of those involved but as said earlier on, how many have been arrested and seriously prosecuted? I am not ignorant of the fact that the persons behind oil theft are highly placed in the society because oil money is big money and big money; can buy big positions in a country like Nigeria where many people are so poor that they still do vote for cash. But my trillion naira question is: must we all go down because of the greed of few men?

Let us see another set of men that has done us evil as a people.

OCCULTISM

Collins Dictionary defines occultism as[14] *1. Believe in the existence of secrets mysterious or supernatural agencies. 2. The study of practice of occult art.* Wikipedia has a much more elaborate definition of the root-word in the word occultism and that is occult[15] – *"The* **occult***, in the broadest sense, is a category of esoteric supernatural beliefs and practices which generally fall outside the scope of religion and science, encompassing phenomena involving other worldly agency, such as magic. It can also refer to supernatural ideas like extra-sensory perception and parapsychology".*

In a nutshell what is outside "religion and science" and is a mystery or it is buried in secrecy is occultism. To prove that something or somebody is occultic is often a very difficult task but one can get a clearer picture when he or she reads the Criminal Code Act of the Federal Republic of Nigeria under the Chapter that is tagged: Unlawful Societies.[16]

Definition of society and unlawful society:

(1)   A society includes any combination of ten or more person whether the society be known by any name or not.

(2)   A society is an unlawful society –

i.   If formed for any of the following purpose:

a)   Levying war or encouraging or assisting any person to levy war on the Government or the inhabitants of any part of Nigeria or

b) Killing or injuring or encouraging the destruction or injuring of any property; or

c) Destroying or injuring or encouraging the destruction or injuring of any property; or

d) Subverting or promoting the subversion of the Government or its officials; or

e) Committing or inciting to acts of violence or intimidation; or

f) Interfering with, or resisting or encouraging interference with or resistance to the administration of the law; or

g) Disturbing or encouraging the disturbance of peace and order in any part of Nigeria; or

ii. If declared by an order of the appropriate commissioner to be a society dangerous to the good government of Nigeria or any part thereof.

The persons that partake in any or all of these atrocities are enemies of any civilized gathering. To this end, the Nigeria Constitution states that the following public offices holder MUST NOT belong to any secret society or occultic group.

i.   President see S.137 (i)(h)
ii. Governor see S.182 (i)(h)
iii. Members of National Assembly see S. 66 (i)(g)

iv. State House of Assembly see S. 107 (i)(g)

I believe that this applies to all other public office holders who may not have been captured in black and white in Nigeria's Constitution. The myriads of evil someone that belongs to an occult group can perform is simply endless and I am certain that; that is the key reason public office holders were barred from joining or belonging to any of such nefarious group. However, it is common knowledge that during general elections in Nigeria, citizens are generally very security conscious because of the mysterious disappearance of individuals – especially virgins. The general belief is that such persons were or are killed by desperate politicians that want political powers at all cost. When a man uses the blood of a virgin he killed to take his bath or goes to a cemetery or big market at night to take his bath, don't you think that some strange evil spirits will overtake his entire being? If he finally gets the post he seeks, he will do things that are totally anit-progress and anti-people because it is no longer him that governs the people but the evil spirits that now possess him. This sadly, has become a recurring decimal in the political landscape of Nigeria.

I know a young man that became the darling of the Local Government Chairman of the community he did his NYSC programme because the later got to know that the former was somehow related to a very prominent politician. He confessed that he got a lot of financial gifts from the Chairman because he asked him to book an appointment for him with his "uncle". The young man was able to fix the appointment between them but sadly, minutes to when both men were to see, the top brass got an emergency call that made him to abruptly leave for Abuja. On the way back to his service station, the Local Government Chairman opened up to him that there was a big post that he wanted badly but he was certain that the powers-that-be at his State level will not give it to him, hence his move to this National figure of the party. He said he was sure that when the National big weight prevails on the State, he will get the position without much trouble. He then asked the young man a question that shocked him. He asked "What is the occult group your uncle belongs to? I don't mind to join them as long as I am assured the position I seek." The young man confessed to me that he was shocked to his foundation and from that moment, he began to distance himself from the Chairman because he reasoned, "if this man can be that desperate, he can as well use me for ritual in order to achieve his aim".

If that man's aspiration is finally achieved when he joins the occult group and he is told to bring a large chunk of State Funds to the group as a mark of loyalty, will he do so in the present Nigeria where serious penalties are not meted to those that steal public funds? The answer is Capital YES. If he is forced to award contract to his fellow cult members and they end up not doing the job after receiving more than 90% of the total cost of the job, will he be bold to call for their prosecution? If he is asked to do a crazy thing like killing a human being, will he do it? The answer is a Capital YES! Demands of this sorts are some of the chief brain behind abandoned projects in Nigeria and they are also part of the reason, public funds at times, develop wings and fly into the pathless cloud. When the blood of the innocent that was shed begins to trouble "His Excellency" and you are talking to him about the economy or some other human concerns, do you think such a person is in the right frame of mind to justly attend to such important public or national matters?

My position is not baseless. If you Google "ritual killing in Nigeria", you will be shocked by what you will find already written by our top newspapers and seasoned journalist.

A case that baffled me till date is that of a 19 year old boy that *Tribune Newspaper* reported.[17] He strangled his biological mother to death and slept with her corpse! He did such bizarre thing because a witch doctor (or voodoo doctor) told him if he carries out the act, he will become stupendously rich. If that young man carried out such terrible act and becomes rich and to make his money "legit" (as they call it), he goes into politics and wins massively after the reckless use of money to buy votes and political stakeholders, what kind of leadership do you think he will give to the people? Someone may want to ask me, what is your business and my quick reply is: if that young man were to be your biological brother, will you clap for him for killing your mum and sleeping with her corpse? Until, without sentiments, we begin to truly scrutinize aspirant of public officers and weed off those that have sold their hearts to the devil and his works, we may be daydreaming of a glorious Nigeria where all round pegs will be put into round holes.

Let see a related group that have not only fast tracked the enthronement of evil men into public offices in Nigeria but has also led to the untimely death of many of our promising youths.

CULTISM

In the simplest form, a cult is a group of people that are devoted to an ideology, a movement, a person or a work and often, they do so with spiritual connotations. But did you know that what we now know as cultism in Nigeria, actually started as a confraternity? The word confraternity simply means a brotherhood, especially one with a religious or charitable purpose. So, how did what is good, turned bad? To do justice to this segment, permit me to quickly state the origin of the oldest student's Confraternity in Nigeria as told by one of its foremost founders – Professor Wole Soyinka. He penned this down in a book titled *Our UI* and I beg your pardon to allow me post a large chunk of his writeup in other to get a better understanding of the entire scenario that lead them to take the step they took:[18]

1952 was the year I finish secondary school and I had written and pass entrance examination to the University College, Ibadan which was only the tertiary institution available in the country then. Before the university session started, I got this job in a medical equipment supply company, where I had this rather prestigious title of senior stores officer grade three! It wasn't that the office environment or even the store itself was something as prestigious as its title; all there was to the business was this huge barnyard kind of warehouse where we stored equipment like catguts, surgical tools and bales of cotton wool among other things. Yes I was enjoying it and had even considered not going into University.

All this soon changed of course, when the admission offer was followed by a Government scholarship. I just could not resist that bait, so I resigned my job as senior store officer grade three, and packed my belongings together to begin my sojourn in University College Ibadan. The University was still at its old site which was nothing but an ex-army barrack at Eleiyele. We didn't stay more than the first year before we move to the new site, on the old Oyo road.

Comparatively, I rather like the old site of the campus

for many reasons, although it was no match for the new site in terms of infrastructural beauty or convenience. While the old site at Eleiyele had a kind of English egalitarian atmosphere, at the new site attempts were made to create a kind of British collegiate atmosphere by the hall Masters.

This means that the students attitude changed from the natural realistic trend of life to assume very unreal and unrealistic colonial dimensions. Class distinctions became the order of the day, and the proliferation of elitist clubs had begun. Huge ballroom dances came into being which you attended in three pieces suits, at which also you wouldn't be caught dead without a tie. Sometimes a brooch was added too, for good measure. I too wore a tie and even the brooch but, I did not take it as seriously as the other students appeared to. Unlike the others, I didn't begin to think too highly of myself. Student then felt they were sort of very special, very privileged people who were separated from the community, and because of this they took some most outrageous decisions.

I recall once that the SRC (student representative council) passed a resolution calling on the Government to remove the railway crossing at Sango because it disturbed them when they were returning from shopping in town or night clubbing at one of the many clubs available in Mokola. I found this very hilarious and very amusing yet it was serious. Students were suffering from a disease I can only summarised as having an overinflated sense of self.

The culmination of this ego trip was the Sigma Club. This was the club's or socially aware, supposedly exposed and sophisticated (more like coloniated) students who were strangers to poverty and had become as near to a white man as the white part of their eyes. They had these parties which were the high point of the social calendar on the campus. They went about, all suited up, even in the most blazing sun and prided themselves on being gentlemanly in their manners and ways, which to me read stiff, aloof and unnatural. Anyway Sigmaites were the conservatives and societal standard of sophisticated beings on campus.

It was not only Sigmaites who were guilty of this disease call *colonial mentality* raging through the University like wildfire. Most of the male students were very chauvinistic. They had this attitude to women which I didn't like. *The Bug*, a campus journal was there mouthpiece. The women on campus then, rather few in number, were bugged mercilessly, cruelly and hopelessly. In vicious vitriolic language, they were made to feel like second-class citizens and pure trash. Some of the women on campus then, include the present Mrs. Ann Ofure and Francesca Emmanuel (who had such a great voice and was very active in the theatre). One of the ladies I can't recall her name now, had a very impressive personality and she was also one of those who constantly wore Yoruba attire. I remember *The Bug* reached its lowest in my estimation, when in one of his editions this lady was bugged. They wrote: *Market woman market woman, Jankoliko market woman Jankoliko.*

They likened her to a rustic illiterate market woman because she dared to wear native clothes! My God! That was the point at which I concluded that this disease should not be allowed to thrive any longer. I mean, how could student who prior to the opportunity of going to university would probably have been no more than farmers or traders get into a campus and change so much, forgetting their humble beginning (some of them were very much below average and couldn't have paid their way through school if they didn't get a scholarship) turn round quickly and call those things which they have always lived up with, were born into, and grown up with, crude, local, unrefined and crass, and call things which they've only been exposed to, for not more than five or ten years as worthy and necessary to give one a veneer of sophistication and worldliness. It only meant, or so I reasoned that the colonialist (the British) had scored a bull's eye. They had won a golden victory by colonizing not only our land but also our minds. Sadly this reversal values, of regarding everything of colonial or white-skinned origin as good and those that were of African origin or substandard quality therefore bad, was the order of the day. The most infuriating aspect of this student colonial mentality was that it had a touch of arrogance in it.

The only way I need to quell this unfair, unabashed trampling of African values and the women's sensitivity was to start another campus journal which we called *The Eagle*. We used it to attack colonial mentality. Some of my friends like Aig-Imoukhuede and Pius Oleghe were my co-editors. *The Eagle* attacked, always, *The Bug's* libellous faces. One thing led to another and it became the precursor of one of the most important relics of my Ibadan association - The

Pyrates Confraternity. Myself, Pius Oleghe, Ralph Opara, Aig-Imoukhuede, Ifoghale Amata, Oyelola and Awe found we were like minds, who were determined to add the letters BA and BSc to our names. Yet we believe that a university education should be fun, without the viciousness which was prevalent on campus. We also thought students should map out a character of their own, rather than follow sheepishly the norms and traits of our large European staff.

One day seven of us got together in somebody's room (whose I can't remember because some of them live next door to me) and said, 'Let's start something'. Everybody was enthusiastic and full of ideas. One person suggested the name, another thought of the attire, another person thought up our initiation ceremony. One thing which we all agreed to was there wouldn't be any room for colonial mentality in the club. Thus the Pyrates Confraternity was born. We were going to be a sort of counter revolution against colonialism.

Our first-ever initiation ceremony took place in a kind of split-level hut behind Tedder Hall. It was a kind of semi bunker (which I guess must have been destroyed now) just on the lawns, and it had a kind of alcove which was raised on a plank. We met there, discussed and held our elections. I was chosen to be the first Captain. We henceforth held our meeting (sailed) there. Although we might have been a little wild, it was not usually due to the influence of alcohol as most people assumed. We didn't drink anything stronger than beer. Our concoction which was one of the symbols of our mystery was just Krola (the soft drink at that time) mixed with beer. Our noisy and boisterous activities were just the letting loose of otherwise restricted and chained instincts of youthful freedom and exuberance. Unlike popular belief also, the Confraternity was not designed to be a secret cult. We sailed in my time, on top of the platform. Our performance which was just singing, telling stories and debating (albeit at the top of our voices) were open to anybody. We discussed everything including politics and anybody who liked and wanted to loosen up was free to join us.

Most of the rites, ceremonies and mystery shrouding the club's activities were later day innovations of future generations who identified with the ideals of the organizations. For example in my time, we didn't have the pyratical language. Our uniforms were not regularised too. Everybody was required to use his imagination and initiative as long as he came out as pyratical as possible. One of my life's greatest thrills is to recall that day seven of us formed the Confraternity, and to remember that it only survived after we left, for it was a phenomenon that spread to and was accepted by other institution in the country. That it made so much impact on the lives of its adherent such that they didn't want to stop being a part of it even after they left their various institutions. That this made them formed the National Association of Seadogs to which graduate Pyrates have shown so much dedication that they have been able to carry out such humanitarian gestures and succeed in some social reforms. This is very commendable and is an issue of pride to me anytime I recall it….

Perhaps the only part of myself I discover in Ibadan was my counter culture person. It was at Ibadan that I realized, and erupted my nonconformist attitude and stance. This led to my participating actively in the thing that gives me the most joy about Ibadan, *The Pyrate's Confraternity*. It has been significant, because even though my stay at Ibadan was short (since I left for Leeds after the inter BA examinations), something which I was a part of has survived the forty so odd years as an enduring part of the University tradition and culture. Although, at some point, later today Pyrates diverted from the initial objectives of the Confraternity which was to counter colonial mentality and to protect the ladies from the undeserved harassment of chauvinistic males (a sort of knight in shining armour). We older Pyrates were invited to come to straighten them out since they had got themselves in things which were downright evil. We came in, probed into the matter, we sunk some of the decks and told others to clean up their act and separate themselves from some of these things which were really evil.

From his narrative about the origin of confraternity activities in Nigeria, it is clear that the thoughts of the founding fathers of the first confraternity group in Nigeria were indeed, very noble. Till date, Prof. Wole Soyinka maintains that it is wrong to lump cultism and confraternity together because both of them are not the same.[19] I totally agree with him because the letter promote brotherhood that protect and promote virtues that makes a society an interesting and peaceful place while the former is a direct opposite. However, in the afore cited write up Prof. Soyinka pened down himself, he stated that "*Pyrates diverted from the initial objectives of the Confraternity which was to counter colonial mentality and to protect the ladies from the undeserved harassment of chauvinistic males ... got themselves in things which were downright evil.*" So, we can clearly see that what started on a sound and pleasant note has sadly, turned sour. Academic brilliance and deep respect for Africa and Africans were the founding ideologies but same cannot be said of what is obtainable today. You really need to use a very good magnifying glass to be able to see anything good in virtually all that concerns the many off-shoots of that group that started many years before Nigeria got her independence on a good note.

Do you know the reason for the substantial deviation? Dominance! Is the key word. Dominance gives "free" money, women and other needs of life that gives "enjoyment" to the body. The struggle for dominance is both intra and inter cult groups. To worsen the whole scenario, politicians or political parties now have cult groups that are loyal to them and do their bidding. In the last gubernatorial election in Edo State for example, several Newspaper houses reported on the accusation and counter accusation of the leading political parties as per the use of cultists to undo the other. For me, cult groups have now become like a mad woman that I used to see roam Dawson Road in Benin City, Edo State. It was an open secret that while she was alive, she had serious money. Her source? Men that needed spiritual powers often gave her money to have sex with her all through the night and in the day, such men would never want to identify with her. She was later found dead in an old building and her corpse had begun to decay before government officials came to evacuate it. Many cult boys have died in gruesome way that is best left imagined. The "Political Leader" that sent them on errand will never be humane enough to pay condolence visit to the family of the deceased because he will never want to be openly identified with the group - just like the case of the late mad woman at Dawson Road.

Are all present day cult boys evil? My answer is a Capital NO. Many got involved before they knew the gravity of what they got themselves hooked up to and they really want to come out but is more difficult to get out than to get in. I once had an interview with an athletic built young man that opened up to me that he was a cultist. He told me one of his ordeals that I can never forget in a hurry. He said they once went to initiate new intakes into their group and as usual, it goes with some rituals and beating the new members. There was a particular young boy that he so dealt with that his colleague asked him if he want to kill the boy or if he had a prior score to settle with him. He said he kept them quiet till date and asked if I know why he did such a callous thing? I responded in the negative and he responded in pidgin and said. *"This place wey men like me dey, we dey think of how we go take come out, na him one small boy wey him papa buy jeans give say make he go school wan come put head"*. Meaning he was tired of the system and wanted a way out, therefore, he did not want the young man to fall into the trap that had held him tight by joining them. He felt if he beat him very well, he would run away and the initiation would be aborted but alas, the young man endured the beating and was finally initiated. When it is now the turn of that young boy to initiate others, what do you think will be his style? This is one of the core reasons cultism gets bloodier by the day in Nigeria. I will end this segment by quoting a portion of an article that is titled: "Blood on the Street! Cultist Go Rampage Killing, Maiming", written by Christian Nwokocha and co. *Saturday Independent Newspaper* of November 21, 2020 published it.[20]

> In the past few weeks, residents of many cities in the country have been living in abject fear as blood litters the streets resulting from gale of killings by rival cult groups. In others, there had been a spike in armed robberies and kidnappings. In Benin metropolis of Edo State, no fewer than 40 lives have been wasted following the reported killing of three more persons on Wednesday night. The prevailing cult clash, which is in its fourth week has taken a new dimension following the shooting and injuring of an Assistant Commissioner of

Police (ACP), Agabi Godiri and two Police Inspectors during an exchange of gunfire with suspected cultists at the notorious Upper Sokponba Road by third junction. ACP Godiri, who is heading Benin Area Command Metro of the Police Command was on his way to answer a distress call at the Upper Sokponba Road end of Benin City, when he was shot at by suspected hoodlums. Our Benin correspondent, who visited the hospital saw the Assistant Commissioner of Police where he is recuperating. It was discovered that the Police Area Commander was injured on his right arm during the attack as he was quick to escape after he was fired at by the ravaging gunmen. Besides the broad daylight gun booms, innocent residents are also faced with incessant robbery, allegedly perpetrated by suspected cultists. At the epicenter of the bloody clash is Upper Sokponba Road in Ikpoba-Okha Local Government, Textile Mill/Ogida/Medical (Egor Local Government) and Isiohor/Oluku/Ovbiogie communities in Ovia North-East Local Government Area …

Delta, the neighbouring state to Edo has not been spared the resurgence in cult killings too. Last week, seven persons were said to have been killed as two rival cult groups clashed in Ughelli, headquarters of Ughelli

North Local Government Area of Delta State. A Point of Sale (POS) Operator was also robbed and shot by hoodlums at the weekend during the clash between Aiye and Bangas cultists, while many others were left with serious injuries as both groups engaged each other with guns and other weapons. Saturday INDEPENDENT reliably gathered that trouble started when one of the members of the cult groups was killed which later led to killings of members of both cult groups. An anonymous source confirmed that over the weekend, several members belonging to each of the groups have been killed at different locations of Ughelli, Ughelli North Local Government area. It was gathered that one of the strongmen of Bangas was murdered along Akpodiete Street, two others killed in Ekiugbo while another one was killed at Oghenevwetata Street on Saturday night. Two other cult members suspected to be brothers, Master Frank and Oghenero, were attacked at their house (Poyo compound) close to Ataverhe junction in Ekiugbo, Ughelli North. Frank and his brother Oghenero were dragged from their room to an uncompleted building within the compound where they were both shot dead, while others received machete cuts on the head and neck regions ... Their stronghold in other parts of South South are Calabar, Port Harcourt and Yenagoa where many lives were allegedly lost resulting from their nefarious activities. They operate with charms, guns, axe, spares and arrows and other dangerous weapons. Saturday INDEPENDENT gathered that in Bayelsa State, cultists on a regular basis cause panic among residents and business operators. The cultists allegedly operate with assault rifles, locally made pistols and other weapons with a view to attack their targets in broad daylight and at nights too. The suspected criminals kill and rob their victims of money, handsets and other valuables even as they use Keke NAPEP to carry out their criminal expeditions in most parts of the state. In some instances, clashes involving rival cult groups had also resulted in the deaths of members and innocent citizens.

Some of the notorious flashpoints in Yenagoa include, Edepie-Etegwe roundabout, Akenfa, Opolo roundabout, Julius Berger flyover, Ovom and Onopa areas as well as the popular Swali Market, Imiringi Road and Tombia-Amassoma Road.

Investigations revealed that most streets in the state capital had been recording cult related cases, while they are fingered in other armed robbery attacks and kidnapping incidents …

Adamu Bashir, a security expert … said the term 'cult' is traditionally used to reference social groups defined by their extreme religious, philosophical or spiritual beliefs focused on a particular personality, object or goal. These groups often use devious psychological techniques to gain and control adherents (high pressure recruiting tactics) and are often characterised by socially deviant practices or novel beliefs. "There is no particular membership size for a cult. The groups can range in size from a few local members to international organisations with millions." He said the recent resurgence of cult-related killings recorded in Edo and Delta States, especially is one intermittent outburst of such groups. He, however, said that effective policing with a good record of intelligence gathering could have handled such spasmodic strikes and save the people the horror they unleash on the society.

When citizen can no longer perform their lawful duties or sleep with their two eyes closed, is that not a serious problem that should give the government of the day serious concern? Just imagine the massive contributions to nation building that thousands of our promising youths that have died in their prime because of cult related matters would have made. What about the many innocent Nigerians that were wrongly killed by cultist. How would their loved one feel? If cult havoc continues like this and the government cannot bring it under control, is this not one of the key signs that Nigeria is at the verge of sliding into the state of being tagged a "Failed State"? The worst is yet to come. Let us visit the next group of persons that has made life hellish for Nigerians and should be a major concern of a people oriented government.

AGBEROS

Did you know that the present day word popularly called Agbero in Nigeria is actually an adulterated Yoruba word – *Ape-ero* - one who calls passengers? Initially, these sets of men were the poorest of the poor who were neither educated nor skilled in a trade. They therefore helped commercial drivers to call passengers for a token. When politicians began to fight dirty in Nigeria's First Republic, this class of persons were their "fighting tools." After such deadly fights, those of them that survived and had access to these "big men" began to lobby for control of one motor park or the other. With "nothing much to lose," quick approvals were granted but with solemn promise that they will remain loyal and always be ready to do the bids of the "*Oga* at the top." With time, these persons were advised to register themselves with the government in order to secure legal backing and have national spread. Today, more than one of such bodies called transport unions exists and they have national spread.

Over the years, these groups have prospered financially and at times, got powers that many uniformed security agents like the Nigerian Police, do not have. Reason? When they carry out their nefarious activities and one reports them to the Police, either the Police will do nothing about it or sadly, the accuser will become the accused. Reason again? It is either the Police are direct beneficiaries of the activities of the Agberos or they dread the wrath of the big politician that "back up the boys". In some States, these Agberos are so powerful that they dine and wine with the topmost citizens of the State. In one of the Western States in Nigeria, Agberos became so powerful that they once impeached the State Governor in a most shrouded circumstance and until date, there has been no reversal of that unfortunate infraction.

Like a million and one other Nigerians, I have had many ugly experiences due to the callous behavior of Agberos. Three cases that stand tall in my mind are as follows:

1. My friend and I attended a burial ceremony in Imo State on the 10th of July, 2020 and that was the period COVID 19 lockdown was relaxed a bit. When the ceremony was over and we were on our way back to Benin via Onitsha, we got to the Motor Park at

Upper Iweka a few minutes after 4 p.m. They said a car carried just three passengers at 2,000 Naira per person. Before COVID-19, it was 5 passengers at 1,000 naira per person. We told them we could only afford ₦1500 and one of the drivers said he will carry us but he will carry four persons as against three. His proposal made sense to us. In a jiffy, we got another passenger. While we waited for the last passenger, luck smiled on the driver. Someone brought a full Second Hand car engine to the park - to be sent to Benin as waybill. Being that the car was a Mercedes-Benz wagon car, the transaction was quickly concluded. It was a few minutes to 7 p.m. when the last passenger finally came. As we were about to leave the park, there was a massive argument between the driver and the Agberos. The total amount they loaded a car was ₦6000 and the Agberos usually charged ₦2,500, while ₦3,500 naira went to the driver. They said because he collected money for the car engine that is to be way-billed to Benin City, they will collect ₦3,500 and the driver must hold on to ₦2,500! Both parties said over their dead bodies will they shift ground. At the end they asked us to find our way. To cut a long story short, we passed through the eyes of a needle to be able to get a vehicle going to Benin City that night and by the time we got there, it was already after 10 p.m. - curfew had begun. We had to look for a nearby hotel to pass the night. If you were in my shoes, what who would you blame for the hell you went through? The driver or the Agberos?

2.   Early December 2017, a company gave me the contract of branding and supplying their end-of-the-year gift items like towels, tea cups, t-shirts, face caps, and so on. I went to Idumota to buy them for reasons that is known to the average Nigerian business man. To charter a cab that day that would convey my goods was difficult. I had to enter one of the big (semi-molue) buses that plied Oshodi-Idumota. Normally then, it was ₦200 per person. That day, all of them without exception began to charge ₦500 - about 150% increase. I needed to get three seats, so instead of paying ₦600, I had to cough out ₦1,500. Everybody on the bus was irritated by the crazy hike in fare. Five persons occupied each row of seats with great discomfort. One of the rows had just four passengers when we left Idumota and when we go to a nearby bus stop, the driver packed the bus to bring in the fifth person that will mark up that row. The four persons occupying the row refused to allow the individual in. The driver and bus conductor became mad with anger and told us that before Agberos allowed them to line up to pick passengers, they made them part with well over ₦10,000 (the exact figure I can't remember now) claiming that it was their "*owo odun*" – "money for Christmas and New Year celebrations". Our individual resentment for the driver and conductor turned to serious pity. Also, I once entered a *Danfo* at Ketu Bus Stop and while the Bus Conductor was making frantic efforts to get the bus filled with passengers, an Agbero came to demand *"Owo ano mi,*

ati eni daa" – "Where is my yesterday and today's money?" The driver told him that he paid that of the previous day and he should collect the one of that day and the Agbero went wild. The curses he rained on the driver and his mother (that of course did not offend him in any way) were terrible and uncalled for. He then rushed to the front of the bus and removed one of the bus windscreen wipers and went also to the side of the bus to remove one of the fancy plastics that was used to beautify the bus and after more curses, he went his way. Demigod! If not in Nigeria, where else on earth can such madness be practised? If you ever encounter their brothers in Onitsha and Asaba, you will know that the wickedness in the heart of an Agbero is not a respecter of tribe. Let me put it better in pidgin English "Agbero for every part of 9ja, na de same Mama born them".

Now come to think of it why should Agberos collect ₦2500 out of ₦6,000 Naira let alone ₦3500 of ₦6,000 naira? The driver buys fuel, repairs the car when there is a break down, risks his life to embark on the journey and faces a lot of other inconveniences while the Agbero has little or no expenses to pick. Those that collected over 10,000 Naira for "Owo odun," did they care if the driver faced any of the aforementioned challenges? If a citizen have such endless might against his fellow citizens and the State is nowhere to defend the lesser fellow, is that not a serious sign of the State slipping into a Failed State? Have you ever witnessed the impurity, callousness, arrogance, brutality and insensitivity with which 90% of Agberos collect money from drivers? Usually, drivers pay when they pick passengers but some Agberos have become so powerful and insensitive that in some locations, they now force driver to pay when they drop off passengers! Where in the world is such madness allowed if not in Nigeria, my father's country?

My friend in Ghana said the government in Ghana increased the price of petroleum products and their Transport Union begged their members not to increase fares because the populace were going through hard times and the drivers all complied. In Nigeria, the government announced sometimes in September 2021, that they will increase fuel by March, 2022 and immediately, prices of transport fare increased virtually in all parts of the country. If it was not the Agberos that initiated the increase, why did their union not make an open appeal to drivers not to increase their fares as did their Ghanaian counterpart? Certainly, our Agberos were the ones that most likely triggered the increase and as I write, the plight of the common man is pitiable – transportation wise. There was scarcity of fuel sometimes in December 2021/January 2022 that led to the increase in petroleum products. Drivers increased their fares by more than 50% and Agbero were super glad about it because, they too increased their daily collections. As I write this chapter in April, 2022, the prices of petrol have reversed to normal but the killing transport fares have not been reversed. Who cares? Is it the politician that wants to use Agberos to further his political ambition that will interfere or the Agbero Union (or their unseen but always interested "God-fathers") whose revenues has tremendously increased that will say a word in condemnation? Nobody speaks for the common man when Agbero issues are brought up - but I am certain God sees and He will act soon.

If the average Agbero is terrible, what do you think of the man he reports to? To be an Agbero Chairman and the fellow has never killed or fight physically and sustain mortal injuries is a great miracle. It is an open secret that whenever there is a change of leadership in a Motor Park, heads must roll? Reasons? It is a seat meant for "strong men" and the "strong money" that goes with the office. In Benin City and many other places, drivers are meant to pay "Chairman Breakfast Food" money in the morning and in the afternoon, they pay "Chairman Lunch" money. These collections are not included in the main collections of the day and all commercial drivers MUST pay. I was shocked to discover that there is a set of drivers that are called "priority drivers". They pick passengers from places has great access to passengers but often, such places do obstruct traffic. Nobody dare challenge them because of one out of two things. Either the driver pays a huge daily amount to the Agbero Chairman's boys or belong to a cult group that the Agbero Park (or Route) Chairman belongs to. The Chairman needs such loyal drivers to keep his seat or do the biddings of their "Oga at the top." But do you think countries like Dubai and other nations that are wooing the world to come invest in their shores will tolerate any of the many aforementioned madness that has become our norms? Is this not yet another indication that Nigeria is fast heading towards becoming a failed state?

Let me sign off this section by sharing a well-researched article that summarizes all I have said so far. It was written by Suzanne Oyebola. Titled: Lagos Agbero Generate Annual Revenue of N123 Billion, Reports Says.[21]

> 'Agberos' in Lagos generate an estimated annual revenue of N123.078 billion amassed from daily road use taxes levied on bus drivers, tricycle riders and motorcycle operators in the state.
>
> This is according to a recent research report by the International Centre for Investigative Reporting (ICIR).
>
> · Each commercial vehicle driver pays at least N3,000 to Agberos as ticket fee.
>
> · There are an estimated 75,000 commercial buses operating in Lagos, according to the Lagos

Metropolitan Area Transport Authority (LAMATA).

· Estimated daily total collection: **N225 million**

· Estimated monthly total collection: **N6.75 billion**

· Estimated yearly total collection: **N82.125 billion**

· Each "Keke NAPEP" rider pays at least N1,800 to Agberos per day.

· There are an estimated 50,000 tricycles operating in Lagos, according to Techcabal.

· Estimated daily total collection: **N90 million**

· Estimated monthly total collection: **N2.7 billion**

· Estimated yearly total collection: **N32.85 billion**

· Each okada rider pays at least N600 to Agberos per day.

· There are an estimated 37,000 okada riders operating in Lagos, according to Motorcycle Operators Association of Lagos State (MOALS).

· Estimated daily total collection: **N22.2 million**

· Estimated monthly total collection: **N666 million**

· Estimated yearly total collection: **N8.103 billion**

The total annual revenue from the three major modes

of transport in Lagos state amounts to **N123.078 billion.**

The ICIR report admitted that these figures may yet be underestimated as daily levies on the transporters are much higher in some parts of Lagos like Mushin, Isolo, Itire/Ikate among others.

Nigerian states with the highest Internally Generated Revenue (IGR) in 2020

· Lagos State recorded the highest Internally Generated Revenue of N418.99 billion, accounting for 32.1% of the total, closely followed by Rivers State with N117.19 billion.

· Other states with the highest IGR in 2020 include Abuja (N92.06 billion), Delta (N59.73 billion), Kaduna (N50.75 billion), Ogun (N50.75 billion), and Oyo State (N38.04 billion).

As the data shows, Lagos Agberos surpassed all other states in revenue generation, beating oil-producing Rivers State by a handsome N5.89 billion naira.

Where is the money?

The report found no trace that much of this revenue gets into government coffers as the money was not accounted for in the state's annual financial statements.

Also, the report revealed that *"although the Lagos State Internal Revenue Service (LIRS) says on its website that 'road taxes' are among the 25 taxes that are collected by the state government....the government agency provides no evidence on the website that road taxes are being collected by the state government."*

The report further revealed that although some of the revenue was being remitted to the National Union of Road Transport Workers (NURTW) and to the rival union RTEAN, the bulk of the money being generated was most likely completing its journey in private pockets.

"The [motor park] chairman takes the huge chunk of the money, shares the rest to his subordinates and leaves little in an account operated by his union," it stated.

Why is the government looking the other way? The general consensus is that the 'Agbero-industry' thrives so well in Lagos because it is backed by powerful politicians who call in return favours to bully opponents and perpetuate violence during elections. It has also been alleged that many of these 'godfathers' are direct beneficiaries of the scheme.

The Lagos state government loses a great deal of revenue annually to these non-state actors. Suffice to say that these monies could have been channelled into critical infrastructure projects in the state.

From the research data, it is also clear that Lagos and indeed Nigeria can function effectively without the need to borrow as much if the nation took the issue of taxes more seriously and plugged holes through which corrupt elements in the system syphon government revenues. Advanced countries with no crude oil resources function efficiently on tax revenues and even give financial aid to Nigeria. Why then is Nigeria's case different?

If non-state actors have access to such crazy amount of funds and commands such powers, what else is left but controlling the State itself? And when Agberos take charge of our Police and Armed Forces, what would be the fate of the nation called Nigeria? These are strong problems that needs to be urgently tackled or we all go down.

Permit me to now state the last set of powerful non-state actors that have done us terrible evil as a people. They are Political God-fathers or simply put - Godfathers.

GODFATHERISM

From my findings, the word godfather refers generally to (i) A man who sponsors a person or child during baptism and promises to guide the individual in the knowledge of God. (ii) Someone who started an art, school of thought or a concept that gained great followership in succeeding years. (iii) A powerful ruthless leader of a criminal group, especially a mafia family.

The second and third definitions are our focus, in the sense that they are inter-related and perfectly apply to what we see in Nigeria politics.

The word Godfather was made popular by a novel titled: *The Godfather* written by Mario Puzo in 1969. The book was acted in 1972 and the movie instantly gained worldwide viewership and adaptations. The picture of Marionette being held and controlled by an invisible hand that is captured on the front cover of the book best summarizes the book.[22] The movie also shows the ruthless extent men go to protect their interest and determine the fate of others.

A look at post-independent Nigeria has shown clearly that many of our political class, perhaps, did not just watch the movie but adapted it as a way of life in order to secure and maintain dominance in the political arena. If you read a book titled *Why We Struck* written by Adewale Ademoyega and take time to meditate on pages 25 to 30, you will be shocked to discover the ruthless styles that some of Nigerian's "founding fathers" adopted in their days in order to gain and maintain dominance. Today, the situation has become worse.

To gain dominance in the Nigeria political arena, three styles are often adopted. The common and easiest way is to be "zombishly" loyal to a political godfather, doing all his legitimate and illegitimate biddings and keeping your mouth shut at all time. This method generates leaders that can hardly think for themselves, let alone think for the people they are expected to lead. So, if the godfathers believe in stealing public funds and the use of violence to gain relevance, what do you expect from their mentee? This style is, sadly, prevalent in Nigeria and that is what has brought us to this sorry state we currently find ourselves.

 The second style is to team up with the second or third cadre of godfathers in that setting to fight the number one godfather. This style, too, has its own demerits. Reasons? Immediately the opposition is able to silence the main godfather, one of the "oppositors", will enthrone himself as the new godfather and begin to do the things he once lamented the disposed godfather was doing amiss. I know of a politician that came to the political scene shouting at the top of his voice "One Man, One Vote", "Say No To Godfatherism." Immediately he got what he wanted, he became more domineering than all that were before him.

The last way to gain relevance is to honestly think on ones feet and proffer solutions to the numerous problems facing the nation at large. Integrity, brilliance, impartiality, doggedness and avant-garde vision are keys virtues such individuals must have at the tip of his/her fingers. This last category is hard to find and that is **"WHO"** Nigeria badly needs now.

If not for the terrible greed that goes with it, political godfatherism is not bad because, just as one finds mentorship in every other field of human endeavor, so is it in the political arena. An experienced mentor do pass the wealth of knowledge he or she has gained over several decades to a mentee in a couple of hours, weeks, months or years. Sadly in Nigeria, this has not been the case because our political godfather's expectations or demands from their godsons, are often anti-progress.

So, what do political godfathers in Nigeria often demand from their godsons?

1. Handsome or crazy monthly remittance from the State purse. At times, their demands are so much that when all the demands are met, the godson will find it difficult to pay workers' salaries or embark on developmental projects.

2. Majority of all appointments must come from the godfather.

3. Juicy contracts that may or may not be executed must be given to the godfather or his representative.

4. Godfather or his representative must be in charge of collection of all revenue of the State and a percentage of the declared sum must go to his coffers. Nobody dares question the declared sum without grave consequences.

5. Outright powers to dictate how far or fast a mentee can rise or climb the political ladder.

6. Total control or elimination of any significant caucus or group that may disrupt the relevance of the godfather or his income.

7. Worship of the wife and children of the godfather by all godsons and an eternal devotion to them (should the godfather bow out of the state of life) is often demanded.

If one man makes the aforementioned demands from another who serves the people and the demands were all granted, what would be left for the people can never be enough to satisfy the needs of the populace, let alone give room for true developmental projects. This malady is often the actual problem with governance in Nigeria. But do you know that most often than not, the godfathers do not make this demand with "ordinary" hands? Many cases can be found on the net where Nigerian political godfathers took their godsons to a shrine or a terrible witch doctors to go swear that he (the godson) will always be loyal to the godfather and do all his biddings without questioning his authority. The fear of the repercussions of breaking the oath is the major reason, many godsons remain docile even in the face of outrageous demands that he knows will paint him really bad in the eyes of the people.

To checkmate the excesses of political godfathers in Nigeria, I believe the best strategy is to completely abolish indirect primaries of all political parties because the power of the godfathers begins to gain momentum when they are, to a large extent, the ones to appoint the individuals that will be the party's delegates to any convention. They also dictate to a large extent who the delegates are to vote for.

Let me make myself clear. If a political party has, for example, five million registered members, Direct Primaries demands that all the five million persons will have to vote for who will be the Party's Presidential Standard Bearer. But for Indirect Primaries, only about three thousand members or less will be elected (or selected) to go represent the five million and at the end, their votes will be binding on the five million persons they represents. You will agree with me that it is far easier to bribe three thousand persons than to bribe five million people. When it dawned on political godfathers that the *status quo* has changed, they will be more humane in their demands, judgment and actions. We can collectively decide to change the narrative by refusing to idolize known political godfathers and aligning ourselves with any political parties that believes in direct primaries (for the aforementioned reasons).

You will agree with me that the Five Monsters (Cabal, Cultism, Occultism, Agberoism and Godfatherism) that I have talked about in this chapter, have truly dealt negatively with us as a nation in no pleasant measure. Let us first and foremost disassociate ourselves from any or all of these monsters and encourage others to do same. Nigeria will be great again when all clean hands are placed on deck and we begin to call a spade a spade.

Turn with me to the next chapter titled: Nigerian Youths: Leaders of Which Tomorrow?

Works Cited

1. https://www.dictionary.com/browse/rule-of-law#:~:text=Definition%20of%20rule%20of%20law&text=the%20principle%20that%20all%20people,GEESES.

2. https://www.merriam-webster.com/dictionary/rule%20of%20law#:~:text=Definition%20of%20rule%20of%20law,uphold%20the%20rule%20of%20law.

3. https://en.m.wikipedia.org/wiki/Rule_of_law

4. https://en.m.wikipedia.org/wiki/Failed_state

5. https://www.premiumtimesng.com/news/3205-jonathan_defends_oil_industry_cabal_says_they_re_good_guys.html

6.https://en.m.wikipedia.org/wiki/Cabal#:~:text=A%20cabal%20is%20a%20group,who%20are%20outside%20their%20group.

7. https://www.britannica.com/dictionary/cabal

8. https://businessday.ng/energy/oilandgas/article/nigerias-daily-petrol-subsidy-hits-n10-1bn-as-oil-surges/

9. https://www.businessamlive.com/on-crude-oil-theft-illegal-refining-and-modular-concept/

10. https://www.thecable.ng/sylva-nigerias-daily-petrol-consumption-figures-are-crazy-opaque-we-need-to-end-petrol-subsidy/amp

11. Okonjo-Iweala Ngozi. Fight Against Corruption Is Dangerous. The MIT Press, 2018, P.35-36, 38-39. 12. https://www.thisdaylive.com/index.php/2022/03/21/avuru-calls-for-state-of-emergency-in-oil-sector-says-80-of-crude-stolen/

13. News Echo. Deadly Monsters in Nigeria's oil kingdoms. Vol. 3. N0. 41. P.1.

14. https://www.collinsdictionary.com/us/dictionary/english/occultism

15. https://en.m.wikipedia.org/wiki/Occult

16. Criminal Code Art. Unlawful Society

17. https://tribuneonlineng.com/why-i-killed-my-mother-slept-with-the-corpse-by-18-year-old-suspect/

18. Soyinka Wole. Our UI. Bookcraft Limited, 1990, P. 58-63.

19. https://www.vanguardngr.com/2015/08/pyrates-confraternity-isnt-a-cult-says-soyinka/

20. Nwokocha Christain, et al. Blood on the Street! Cultist Go Rampage Killing, Maiming. Saturday Independence, 21 Nov. 21, 2020, P. 14-15.

21. https://nairametrics.com/2021/07/22/lagos-agberos-generate-more-annual-revenue-than-35-nigerian-states/

22. https://en.m.wikipedia.org/wiki/The_Godfather_(novel)

Chapter Two

NIGERIA YOUTHS: LEADERS OF WHICH TOMORROW?

> **Neither the wisest constitution nor the wisest laws will secure the liberty and happiness of a people whose manner are universally corrupt**
> **- Samuel Adams.**

A youth is basically one that is neither a child nor an adult. It is, therefore, the period between childhood and adulthood. The UN says youth are persons between the ages of 15 and 24 years.[1] It is often regarded as the beginning of the period called the Prime of a man's life and that is when a man's physical strength, intellect, enthusiasm, vigor, etc is at its peak. In Nigeria, the term "youth" is ambiguous because, when the opportunity to make or get money pops up, even a man of 80 years will claim to be a youth. It was against this backdrop, I once wrote a play I titled *Our Youths Have Gone Mad Too*.[2] It talks about three candidates that were vying for the post of the President of All Progressive Niger Delta Front. Their age difference is large (79, 45 and 27 years). Each of them claims to be a youth. Their real "persons" were finally let out of the bag during a press debate that turned sour. It is a must-read.

About four decades ago when I was in primary school, I began to hear that "youths are the leaders of tomorrow." Till date, many of the names we then used to hear our fathers talk about as being prominent in the society are still the persons that we keep hearing about and there seems to be no willingness on their part to leave the stage so that true youths that are in their prime can move this country forward with the vitality that is inherent in them. When old men are in charge, they will do "old" things in sluggish ways and there can never be tremendous progress in such circumstances.

A lot has been said about the Nigerian youth in recent past by diverse kinds of persons within and outside the country. One of such comments that is worth mentioning is that of President Muhammadu Buhari. In April 2018, Samuel Ogundipe of Premium Times wrote an article he titled: Buhari Criticises Nigerian Youth As Lazy, Uneducated. The following is a portion of that article:[3]

> President Muhammadu Buhari on Wednesday criticised the attitude of some Nigerian youth, saying they were only hustling to get on the gravy train.

> "More than 60 per cent of thc population is below 30, a lot of them haven't been to school and they are claiming that Nigeria is an oil producing country, therefore, they should sit and do nothing, and get housing, healthcare, education free."

> Mr Buhari was quoted as saying by The Cable during a panel appearance with world leaders at the Commonwealth Business Forum in London. The president's comment adds to an earlier one he made criticising Nigerian youth. During a February 2016 interview with UK Telegraph, Mr Buhari said some Nigerians in the UK, mostly youth, are disposed to

criminality and should not be granted asylum there. He was fiercely criticised for the comment, with many saying it failed to convey the reality of Nigerian youth's exploits. Early this year, an analysis by Rice University in the U.S. showed that Nigerian youth are the most educated of all migrants in the country. The institution credited the finding to a culture of relentless drive for education amongst Nigerians. Only on Tuesday, Vice President Yemi Osinbajo was in Lagos to meet young innovators at Andela and the larger tech community in Yaba. The hub is driven by young innovators and entrepreneurs and is widely seen as a manifestation of their entrepreneur zeal. Mr Osinbajo had also witnessed Nigerian youth's quest for gainful employment in the way they embraced the administration's N-power programme which paid as low as N30,000 a month for teaching jobs.

The aforementioned speech of Mr. President went viral and many social Media platform and some Media Houses reported that the President said "Nigerian youths are lazy". When I heard it, I was filled with mixed feelings. If the report had said the President said "Some Nigerian youths are lazy" I would have recommended that the President be made the life Patron of Nigerian Youths. Reason?

Some Nigerian youth are truly lazy and I will make my position clear with the following examples.

1. When I was in my final year at the University, I was reading in one of our big lecture halls, when one of our lecturers came into the hall with all the 200 level students offering his course. He wanted them to write their semester test. They were more than a hundred students. Immediately he sighted me, he asked me to help him invigilate them. He was at the front of the hall and I was at the rear. I noticed that one of the students did not bend down his head to write anything from the beginning of the 30 minutes test till the end. He was busy spying what others wrote, whether correct or not. I was irritated and asked him "Do you mean you are studying an engineering course and you did not bother to prepare for your semester test? With carefree boldness he said in pidgin English, "Bros, no be everybody wey dey here wan go school oh! Some of us wan jand" - meaning – "Not everybody in this class wants to study engineering, some people want to travel abroad for greener pasture". I then told him "Some dey Jand, dem go do bad things and end up in jail and some dey jand, and dem dey work for better office and dem dey pay them better money, which of the two you wan be? – "Some travel abroad to do illegitimate things and end up in jail while some travel abroad and work in a good office and they are well paid. Which of these two category do you want to belong to?" He said, "E no matter, so far

as man jand" - Meaning he wants to travel abroad without education or skills and he is ready to do illegitimate things to survive when he gets there. When I saw his unbending wrong mindset, I held my peace. Is it not the attitude of such ill-mannered "lazy" youths that do give Nigeria bad names internationally? Many of them can be seen in various prisons of the world and it is all due to the fact that they believe they can get rich quick without being diligent in a legitimate field of endeavour.

2.   I want to do business in Lagos and was sad to see first-hand what some Nigeria youths were doing to a fellow Nigerian youth. A business owner had a Lister generator that had given him serious headache for a long time. He decided to sell it and buy a new one. Fortunately for him, he got a buyer at a price that is a far cry from it true worth. On the day he was to use a Hiab Truck to move the generator from his office to the preferred place of the new owner, youths of the community came out *en mass* and requested that he must buy beer for all of them or he should forget about moving the generator. My take is: where were they when he battled the challenges of the generator all alone? Why should he part with the little change he got from the sale of the generator when he will still have to (perhaps) borrow to enable him buy a new one? If he gives them money for beer and fold up, is that not a huge loss for the economy of the whole community? I also know

of a similar case where a manufacturing company in one of the South-South states of Nigerian, left their building and many investments and relocated to a new community in South East Nigeria. Reason? The youths don't want to work in the company but on a weekly basis, they made demands that the company was finding very difficult to keep up with. The traditional ruler of the community was said to be particularly notorious in his weekly demands. Now that the company has moved out of their community to another, who lose? If youths in Dubai and other developed nation constantly dole out outrageous demands to their foreign investors, do you think they will record the tremendous achievements they are known for? If without doing any kind of work, some youth have the power to demand money from others and such an ugly developments has now become a norm, what will happen if the person or persons being exploited decides to stop working and in turn look for other persons he/they we collect free money from? Remember that even in Freetown, there is no free food.

3.   In 2014, I and a couple of other dignitaries travel to Zambia to witness the wedding of a dear friend that married a Zambian. Honestly, we were all thrilled by the attitude of the people to work, irrespective of the work - white collar or blue collar. Gardeners and other artisans that we saw were seen happily doing their work. If you asked a waitress to get you 10

different items at 10 different times in a quick successions, she would bring the tenth delivery with the same lovely smile that she brought the first. When we returned back Nigeria, all of us that made the trip from Benin City talked highly of the attitude of the people towards work all through our journey from Lagos to Benin City aboard a God is Good Motors chartered bus. When we got to a place called Ore to freshen up, we went to the restrooms and we were welcomed by the harsh tone of the young man employed to keep the toilet clean. "Make una no piss anyhow for there oh. I just clean am now, now" – meaning "Don't get the facility messed up. I just got it tidied up." A friend that is a senior lawyer replied him "No be wetin dem dey pay you for be dat?" meaning "Is that not the reason you were employed and are being paid?" The young man snapped back at him. "I no blame you. Na because you see me for here na him give you mouth to take talk to me anyhow " meaning "I don't blame you. You could talk to me because you met me in my place of work." The Lawyer was irritated and asked him "You reach the most junior lawyer for my chamber for anything?" meaning "Are you by any means, up to the standard of the most junior Lawyer in my Chambers?" We had to intervene when we noticed that the handshakes were extending to the elbow. This incident triggered the talk of the attitude of the Zambians towards work the more when we continued our journey. Apart from a few persons that were born with a silver spoon, most great men today, have a hard tale to tell of their humble beginnings. Failure to appreciate that stage of a man's life often leads many person to commit terrible crimes that will either cut short their lives or make them regret at older age. There is dignity in labour and one should be happy and proud of any legitimate means of making money. Many persons in Nigeria don't see life this way. They are never happy with the work they do at the moment, as long as it does not give a picture that they have broken even financially. Some dare brag "I no get joy" at any slight provocation and for them, that is a good way to act in the public to command respect but for me and any sane mind, such a fellow is not to be trusted with any serious responsibility. What do you think?

4.   Did you see the viral video of the five Nigerian youths in Lagos that all wore adult pampers to a commercial bank and queued up to access the ATM? Literally all of them had a bag that was dangling on their waist region and the bag's carrier hung on their neck. If you are used to the new happenings amongst our youth, you will not find it difficult to put the jigsaw of what triggered their action together. They must have most likely visited a witch doctor that told them that if they dressed like that to an ATM machine in the daytime and possibly recite some incantations, the ATM would cough out all the money in its vault. If all our youth now do is to rely on witch doctors to help them

gain access to quick money, don't you think we have a massive problem in our hands? Don't you know that the effort of the youth of the nation where the ATM machine was manufactured was required for the machine to be produced in the first place before it was bought and brought to Nigeria? Why can't our youths think of how to manufacture ATM machines or other types of machine and struggle to make them household worldwide name? I know the odds against such moves are heavy but go read the history of many world-class manufacturing outfits of today. They all had humble and rough beginnings. The only thing on earth men start from the top is the grave. The lack of this knowledge or the "get success fast syndrome" that has possessed a number of our youths, have gave rise to the notorious "Yahoo plus" thing that has made life unsafe virtually for everybody in Nigeria. Have you noticed the speed at which many of our youth make stupendous money today and die off tomorrow? The madness has become so pronounced, that the House of Representatives has asked the Executive Arms of our government to declare ritual killing a national emergency that deserves an immediate attention[4]. Be honest, who are the majority of persons that are involved in ritual killings in Nigeria? Youths!

But do I completely blame the Nigerian youth for the plight he finds himself? My answer is a capital NO. When without any visible means of livelihood someone goes into politics and the next moment, he owns all the choice houses in town and drives the best cars in the neighborhood, what influence do you expect a young mind to draw from it? When those that study hard and genuinely graduated with good grades can't get government or corporate jobs because they don't have "long legs" and a dunce get good jobs and calls the shot because he/she is related to one politician or the other, how do you convince the diligent fellow that hard work pays?

When a hard-working Nigerian youth establishes a business and electric power failure, poor roads, multiple taxation from official and unofficial quarters, insecurity, throat cutting interest rates and so on, kills the business, should he or she be called lazy? It takes one with a lion heart to graduate from a Nigerian higher institution and decide to venture into entrepreneurship within our shores. I am one of such lion-hearted Nigerians. I graduated in 2003 and rounded off my service year in 2004. I have been self-employed from that time till this moment that I write this book. I shared one of my ugly experiences in business in my previous book, *To Serve Nigeria Is Not By Force* in the chapter that talks about Electric Power. Another experience I want to highlight is the one I had in 2012. I needed N700,000 for a project and hoped to pay back both interest and capital in 3 months. None of the Commercial Banks I approached was willing to play ball. A smooth tongue marketer from one of the Microfinance Banks in Benin City; then told me they will loan me the money if I met their requirements. Their interest rate was 37% per annum and I was to operate the account for a month to demonstrate my financial abilities and lastly I must provide a landed property with a building as a collateral. After I met all these requirements, they said I must go bring the document of a car that is worth more than N700,000 as added collateral. At that point, I gave up and looked elsewhere for funds that enabled me to achieve my set goals. If I had gone ahead to get the documents of a car and collected the money, don't you think the pressure of failure to pay back in 3 months' time could drive me insane? If youths in some climes get easy access to loans at less than 10% per annum and the Nigerian youth get access to loans at between 27 and 120% per annum, will it be fair to call a hard-working Nigerian youth lazy?

Nigerian youths are also confronted with the disease of wasted years due to ASSU strike. When I got admitted into the university in 1997 and filled the column "Expected Year of Graduation" in my fresher's form as 2001 – (a year after the then dreaded "Millennium Year" and the almighty "Millennium Bug"), I felt the years I will be spending in school were too much. Little did I know that ASUU strike will add two solid extra years to it. By the mercies of God, my colleagues and I managed to graduate in 2003 as against the initial 2001. Do you know the gravity of "wasting" two years of the active life of most Nigerian youths on the altar of disagreement between lecturers and the government over matters that in most cases, the latter is to be blamed? Someone cracked a good but sad joke that got me really laughing. He said a White Man asked his Nigerian friend "What is meaning of ASUU Strike?" The Nigerian told him that it is an annual festival in his country! This "annual festival" is making students lose interest in anything academics, have wrong ideology about governance and waste their precious active years to our nation and humanity at large. For God's sake, it has to stop because it is often more difficult to change a bad orientation than to inculcate a good one. So, if the Nigerian youth is not patriotic, the Nigerian government may have hand in it.

How do you preach patriotism to youths that cannot see an atom of patriotism in a good number of our leaders? As a passive member of an online platform called Nairaland, I once read the story of a young Nigerian that once represented this country as an athlete. He left Nigeria to Britain and joined the British Navy. The reason for his action was stated. He had serious health challenges and he made it known to our Sport authorities. Nothing was done to assist him. Even if some money was assigned, do you know that the person that signed it may have pocketed the lion share and the person that was asked to go give him the money, might have as well, pocket the rest and at the end, all the parties involved kept mute and did go scot free? When the young man managed to leave Nigeria, he quickly threw away his loyalty to Nigeria. Not one of all the persons that commented on his action blamed him. Rather, some persons gave more facts to justify his actions and for me, it shows that many persons are becoming sick and tired with the way government officials treat Nigerians. Things in Nigeria have become very bad. If Rashidi Yekini – (the man that scored the first goal Nigeria ever recorded at world cup) was neglected and he died in sorrow, only for numerous award and contributions to pour in after his death, tell me why should the Nigerian government expect a Nigerian youth to risk any part of his or her body to bring glory to her? We must change these ugly narratives pretty soon. Let me show you a practical way to teach patriotism as can be found in Chinua Achebe's small, powerful and sadly, still relevant book titled *The Trouble with Nigeria.*[5]

> National pledges and pious administration administered by the ruling classes or their paid agent are entirely useless in fostering true patriotism. In extreme circumstances of social, economic and political inequalities such as we have in Nigeria, pledges and admonitions may even work in the reverse directions and provoke rejection or cynicism and despair.
>
> One shinning act of bold, selfless leadership at the top,

such as unambiguous refusal to be corrupt or tolerate corruption at the fountain of authority, will radiate powerful sensations of well-being and pride through every nerve and artery of national life.

I saw such phenomenon on two occasions in Tanzania in the 1960s. the first was when news got around (not from the Ministry of Information but on street corners) that President Nyerere after paying his children's school fees had begged the bank to give him few months grace on the repayment of the mortgage on his personal house. The other occasion was when he insisted that anyone in his cabinet or party hierarchy who had any kind of business must either relinquish them or leave his official or party position. This was no mere technicality of putting the business interest in escrow but giving it up entirely. And many powerful ministers including the formidable leader of TANU Women were forced to leave the cabinet. On these occasion ordinary Tanzanians seemed to walk around, six feet tall. They did not need sermons on patriotism; nor a committee of bishops and emirs to inaugurate a season of ethical revolution for them.

I am glad that despite the many uphill challenges against the Nigerian youth, tens of millions of them are still treading the path of diligence, integrity and world class innovations. The article I first cited in this chapter, tells us that the Vice President of the Federal Republic of Nigeria, Prof. Yemi Osibanjo was excited to identify himself with the ingenious works of some Nigerian youths. To all such visionary, world-class minded, dogged, honest and hard-working Nigerian youths, I say in the Spirit of Aluta, seven hearty "Gbosas" to their efforts! These are the class of persons that this nation is eagerly looking up to for industrialization, direction and innovation. It is the responsibility of a purposeful government to create an enabling environment for them to do so. Permit me to cite several portions of a book I have read religiously because of the massive truth and practicality that it contains. It is entitled: *MY VISION Challenges In The Race Of Excellence* by Mohammed bin Rashid Al Maltoum - Vice President And Prime Minister of United Arab Emirates and ruler of Dubai. The under quotes best summarizes all I have said so far in this chapter:[6]

> Dubai is not the place for people who are strong and healthy, but have no contribution to make, or are simply not prepared to work hard for success. There are always those who need help in every community – and these people will receive help in Dubai – but the rest must make wake up early, race, trade, manufacture, produce, build and make profits, in an atmosphere of positive

competition, security and hope, because it is what Dubai is about. - P. 39,40.

You must give to be allowed to take. To accumulate talent, you must develop it, to make a good trainer, you must train someone first; to make leaders, you must coach promising talents and teach them how to avail themselves of good opportunities and avoid failure. – P.59.

Sheikh Zayed taught us that leaders who genuinely wants to improve the status of his people realizes the importance of training human resources and equipping them with the right skills and expertise, so that they carry out their task efficiently and successfully. He is the one who instructs government departments to prepare and implement the plan needed to achieve these goals. Managing developments is after all, the process of managing people. - P.60.

The quality of a group is derived from the quality of his members, and the strength of a community is derived from the strength of his sons and daughters. When we free the potential of individuals, we simultaneously free the potential of all the community they are part of, and when we let the creativity of individual blossom, the creativity of the whole community blossoms. This is no big secret. When we are facing development issues that need us to run in order to successfully face them, how can I expect anyone to run if I keep putting obstacle in their way? ... What is the use of encouraging a soldier to fight when you have not trained and armed him properly? - P.94.

The mission of the government should be to promote its people creativity and to understand that continuous humiliation, degradation and criticism stifle creativity. How can people be creative when they are afraid or frustrated? When bureaucracy is rampant, corruption is widespread, equal opportunity simply does not exist and most jobs and promotions are obtained through powerful people – you have a situation that leaves people with no hope for the present or the future. This environment produces a totally demoralized citizen who cannot achieve any of his goals, one who cannot even dream about a better future because he is afraid of face the bitter reality when he wakes up each morning. You simply cannot kills the power of dreaming in young people and then ask them to be creative and excel. If you kill the dream, you kill hope; and if you kill hope, what kind of life will be left for people to live? It is as only normal for young people to feel pessimistic and frustrated when they become entrapped in such a situation. And since young people who do not own anything have nothing to lose, they lose interest in everything. - P. 116.

I have said it before and I will say it again: people are the most important ingredient of the development process. If we fail to educate young people, develop their skills and generate the spirit of excellence and creativity in them, we will never, under any circumstances, have a successful development process. - P.129,130

I am convinced that teaching our children the same way we did yesterday is in itself perpetuating a new kind of illiteracy that no longer has a place in any society that wishes to join the global race. Success in this race calls for educating new generations – who believe in God and realize their commitment to their nations – in all kinds of modern discipline, to qualify them to compete globally in various fields of modern science. We can only achieve this by upgrading our education systems, gearing our teacher with the latest tools, using modern technologies in education, and providing a dynamic academic environment that promotes scientific research, innovations and creativity in compliance with an advanced, practical and all-inclusive strategy that prioritize education as a vital pillar of our nation's comprehensive development plan. - P.196

From the quotes above, do you now understand why Dubai and many other nations are doing well and we are not? When irrespective of tribe or creed, we truly create the right environment for all youths in Nigeria, then, we will be shock to realize the massive human potentials that God has blessed this country with. Then, we will have youths that are truly the leaders of tomorrow because they will be able to proffer solutions to the present and future challenges that that confronts us as a nation.

I want to end this chapter on a note that is not pleasant because it is the stake reality (as at the time of writing this book) that we find ourselves as a nation. I pray that this ugly narrative will be phased out pretty soon. My friend and course mates, Engr. Dr. Festus Owu wrote a book he titled: *Laying On The Dagger's Tip*. Being a grassroots politician with more than two decades experience, he exposed the ills that are prevalent in our present political structure. Chapter Five of that book is titled: The Irony of A Super Slave. Permit me to borrow leaf from the said chapter:

> " On rear occasions and particularly, when the services of a tenant profits the landlord above rentage and indulgence of the tenant, tenantship could be exciting and comfortable. Ironically, if the boundaries of this

comfort is not properly defined, it may yield a dangerous fantasy that presupposes that the tenant is not injectable and ascribe heirship under intense hallucination. The fortune of rentage and the tolerance of offensive indulgence though account for comfort, but the defining factor of the length of stay is predicated on the resourcefulness of the tenant. The catastrophe in this seemingly saprophytic relationship, is that the tenant losses the opportunity of status change from tenant to landlord through wrongly invested resources and stands against reality that holds that, tenant ship does not translate to ownership.

The super slave nomenclature runs the content of its portfolio on this falsehood. It gives a wrong notion that, since a particular slave enjoys a level of closeness to the slave master and enforces the decision of same on the larger slave society, that such a slave is super in nature. This is an illusion that describes naivety and bareness of the sound doctrine of logical reasoning. The qualifying word 'super', does not tell less of a slave, but rather conveys a sense of mockery of one who, not only has acclimatized, but also, has foreclosed any ambition to secure freedom and independence. The slave master harps on this wrong deposition and further reinforces it with some incentives that allows for the thinking of a king in the kingdom of the lepers, which is only achievable when the king is first a leper for effective leadership. The journey to this state of absolvent of the slave, begins with the slave masters identification of followers, who possess the requisite zest and oratory prowess or the force of brutality with antecedence of crime and criminality to push the master's ideology through turbulent times and resistance to actualization... A common tactical gimmick by the slave master in retaining the fire power of the super slave, irrespective of their mode of enlistment and their compelling approach, is that they are all promised the slave empire. As they assume that this will be the case in the long run, time begins to fail them as the ineffectiveness of old age pitches them against the vibrancy of ambitions. Of course, this wish to inherit the empire is not superficially wrong, as a labourer is entitled to the right wages, but it is a tall order with the slave master, who sees such covetousness as an affront and a misplaced request for an unsolicited retirement. Conscious of the fact that the super slave will demand this right with time, they fall deeper as they grow in strength into a power play that is fashioned by the slave masters to create a diversionary challenge that consistently keep them in an endless search…The later description is insightful enough in exposing the super slave to mean a greater victim of slavery than the ordinary slave, since super slavery is an all-round entanglement that involves even rational and emotional will power. The achievement of this total control over the errand slave is the reason for the easy enforcement of the skewed 'no better home than this ideology', where the said home reflects total discomfort and extreme squalor. The dishonor in licking a dirty boot, which is constantly the quality of any bad leaders' boot and the oppression of singing the praise of one's tormentor in chief, lays credence to the sorry state of the super slave. The sufficiently indoctrinated slave feels threatened, thinking outside the box and remain restricted to the fettered circle of slavery, for the fear of survival in the larger society outside the bread of sorrow that super slavery have to offer

From the above portion of that great book, the following can be deduced

I. A number of Nigerian youths have made themselves slaves to politicians that have in turn, made them docile in their thinking and as such, carry out their ill orders without questioning or thinking.

ii. These youths are made to believe that the peanuts they get from their Political Masters is the best they can get out there and that makes them to be glued to their slave master's apron.

iii. These political godfather make them to live only for "now.". They massively encourage riotous living - sniffing or smoking hard drugs, drinking oneself to stupor, engage in illicit sex, clubbing and so on. When the aforementioned is all a man live for, how on earth can he be productive? I saw the writing on the shirt of a Nigerian youth and that it got me worried for days. What was written on it?

EAT

SLEEP

PARTY

REPEAT

If this is all that youths in China and other fast-growing economies live for, will their countries be advanced in science and technology by now?

iv.   Sadly, such youths are configured to abhor the word INTEGRITY. They are configured to believe one is smart when he or she is dubious to all apart from the Master that did the configuration. Such men don't tolerate any of their "super slaves" that tries to steal from them or outsmart them. Yet, they train them to use violence or treachery to obtain things from others. In such dens, the rule is: Be Smart But Never Attempt To Outsmart The Master.

v.   The slave master encourages his loyalist to do things that runs foul of the law and "provide" cover for same for as long as he/she remains loyal. But in the true sense, the Slave Master achieves two things by so doing. Firstly, it makes the super slave unfit for any public office and secondly, the super slave is always reminded that failure to carry out further deadly assignments will automatically lead to exposure of his past deeds. Hence the master is always sure he will have his way with the super slave irrespective of how dirty the assignment is.

vi.   Any attempt to go for higher education or be productive in a trade that will make the super slave ever able to compete or challenge the authority of the slave master is often resisted by the latter. To give constant daily hand-outs that will make the super slave always dependent is ever welcome but to give such the super slave a lift that will forever make him independent is a taboo that the slave master will never tolerate. If he ever allows a leverage, it is such that will never allow independence of the super slave.

A friend once told me the story of a known Political Slave Master that never support the "have" and ever ready to support the "have not." To justify how "kind" the self-centered man is, he told me this story about him to "justify" his views. He said, a man that is an artisan and possibly, can barely read or write, was privileged to meet the Political Godfather or Slave Master and he begged him to massively support one of his friend that contested for the post of Local Government Chairman in the previous election and lost. The godfather asked him *"Why don't you rather beg me to make you the Local Government Chairman?"* The artisan quickly jumped at the offer and was not only made the Local Government Chairman but one of the super slaves of the godfather. What was the leverage the godfather was looking for by such "kind gesture" that certainly will never benefit the people of that Local Government Area? Eternal loyalty!

7. The word slave remind me of a film that I once watched that is titled: Roots. It was written by Alex Haley and premiered in 1977. It talks about a young man called Kunta Kinte that was stolen from Gambia at the age of 17 and sold into slavery and his buyers took him to America. He refused to let go of his "Africanness" and made attempt to run away from his Slave Master four times. At the fourth attempt, he was given two options: be castrated or lose half a foot. He chose the latter option and that option is the best for his posterity but it confined him to (in the exact word of Engr. Dr. Festus Owu) - "No better home than this ideology." The two nasty options the Slave Masters gave Kunta Kinte is the same with the options I see many political godfathers give to not only

their super slaves but the entire Nigeria populace. "You can't have more than three kids because the economy is bad" they yell at us but they have numerous wives and concubines that "hatch" a long list of children for them. Some of such children are discovered only after their demise. Our legs are also "cut off" in the sense that, the Super Slaves or the majority of the populace, finds it difficult to go on vacation, travel abroad for medication or studies as we see many political Slaves Masters and their children often do. I STRONGLY BELIEVE, that's if the resources of this blessed nation are judiciously used, there is more than enough to give all Nigerians the best of life they all deserve without taking any of the options presented to Kunta kinte.

8. They encourage the superlative slave to lay their lives on the line by joining a notorious group that will assist them get their desired public office by hook or by crook. In a book titled *Election Violence In Nigeria: A New Perspective* written by Barr. Mrs. Gloria Egbuji, one is made to understand that, it is the Youths that mainly partake in election rigging, violence and hijacking of ballot boxes. Permit me to quote her[9]:

> Evidence abound in the Southern part of the country in particular where politicians who belong to one cult group or the other with the sympathy of a cult group usually resort to the use or support of such group to pursue their political ambition. Members of cult group

easily become willing tools in the hands of their sponsor or patrons who want to acquire political power by all means. They normally resort to rigging, hijacking of ballot papers, kidnapping or Killing of opponents prior or during election or causing a breach of peace during casting of votes if it is feared that their candidate would not secure victory at the polls in a free and fair atmosphere.

A repentant cultist as cited earlier in one part of this book, on behalf of his colleagues during their renunciation of cultism and at Badagry in March 2018 had explain how politicians took advantage of the joblessness and violent attribute of cult members for their selfish political ambition during elections. The cult boys were employed to cause breech of peace during elections once their sponsors seems to be losing.

With increase in cult-related activities in some part of the country and the willingness of jobless cultist to offer their services for money during election, the possibility exists that cult war could jeopardize the chances of having a non-violent electoral process. In Lagos State alone, over 800 suspected cultists have been arrested by the police between 2017 and 2018.

When such Slave Masters through violence get into the corridor of power, what do you expect of them other than further violence and embezzlement of public funds? It seriously pains me that these days, many youths cheaply offer themselves to Slave Masters as political thugs and don't care to die to defend a man that will never allow his biological children to be hurt by a fly. The Nigerian Youth must wake up and wise up, NOW!

I will finally draw the curtain on this chapter by telling a story I read in a motivational book about 20 years ago. I wish I can remember the title of the book for proper referencing but because of massive impact the story had on me and I believe same will be made on every Nigerian youths that buys this truth the story conveys, I can't let go of the story but pen it down here. It talks about an expert American criminal that specialises in robbing very wealthy Americans. He robs persons that have multiple security aids, vicious dogs, advance safe and all manner of other security set up that are very difficult to beat. He often spend quality time to understudy his potential victim and when he is done, the best security network falls like a pack of card before him. He was so good at what he was doing, that it became a thing of secret pride on the part of the victim that the man came to rob him because he will immediately be rated a very healthy man by the America Press. Nothing last forever, especially crime. Someone finally give the police a tip that eventually led to his arrest. He was sentenced to prison for many years. He served the prison term and afterwards, relocated to Britain. He began to live a quiet life that is completely void of crime. A lady that knew his past exploit saw him and alerted the community about him and with one accord, they agreed to make him the head of their security network. An offer he accepted after serious persuasions.. He did his new work so well that a curious reporter went to grant him an exclusive interview. He asked him a lot of questions and reserves the best for the last. He asked him "of all the people you robbed, who did you rob the most?" The answer to the question is meant for the headlines. "ME" was his unexpected answer but when asked what the rationale behind his answer was. He said, he realised that if he had used all the intelligence and energy he used to rob others to start up a business empire, he would have become very successful and would not have spent a large chunk of his life in prison.

To be candid, the average Nigeria is very intelligent and can be very hard-working if he or she chooses to. My position stand solidly on his two legs when you consider the fact that a good number of Nigerians that live abroad are top brass in any field of endeavour the venture into. Back home, you will appreciate the hustling spirit of the Nigerians when you consider how ordinary Nigerians go extra mile to provide water, electricity, roads and other things for themselves when the government fails to do so.

As earlier said, the bad examples of many of our political class, are what has triggered complacency and criminality in the minds of some of our youths. I want Nigerian youths to know that the golden and timeless truth from the aforementioned story is this: WHAT LIVES INSIDE OF YOU IS FAR GREATER THAN WHAT LIVES AROUND YOU! This is the true secret of true greatness.

Permit me to post two of my poem that best address this chapter. They are titled: 9ja Youths: Is Your Brain Paining You? and Mental Slavery.

9JA YOUTHS: IS YOUR BRAIN PAINING YOU?

Mugabe The Great asked this rhetoric question:
Is your brain paining you?
Osiriame The Poet toes his line of thoughts to ask 9ja Youths:
Is your brain paining you?
He highs himself with a bottle of wine that costs N2.5 million
And highs you with Monkey Tail of N25
Is your brain paining you?
His children return from abroad to get good jobs
And you return from prison to get another "Big Job"
Is your brain paining you?
He kills his political enemies with a gun
He placed in your hand

And you are hiding from the police while
He is smiling on TV
Is your brain paining you?
His children run his errands to his associate in the day
And you run his errands to his deadly opponents in the night
Is your brain paining you?
He travels to different countries of the world to enjoy himself
And come back to show you the pictures and you shout
"*Twale* Baba. Enjoyment Master."
Is your brain paining you?
His children spent 4 years or less in Ivy schools
And you spent 12 years in 9ja Uni
Working for him and being expelled and
Working for him and being expelled and
Working for him and being expelled
Is your brain paining you?
You carried ballot box for him and almost got killed
And he carried State Funds and lives like a king
Is your brain paining you?
His phones are always with his PA that always tells you
"He is in a meeting"
But now that elections are here
He calls you by himself and you rush to meet him
Guy, Is your brain paining you?

He then pays you N20, 000 to vote for him
Thereby settling you for 4 years of his tenure
At N13.69k per day.
For God's sake, is your brain paining you?

This *mumurism* **MUST STOP!**
If he has a "Big Job" to execute
Let him be at the front
And let his sons be the next behind him and then
You will follow them
After all
I'm sure your brain is not paining you
9ja Youths: I Hail!

MENTAL SLAVERY
Bob Marley timelessly echoes
Emancipate yourself from mental slavery
None but ourselves can free our minds
Osiriame The Poet sees a lot of lies
Many people worldwide - especially Nigerians
have swallowed that badly limits them
Until the day they bow out of the stage of life

None can change the narrative except Self

You were born into a poor family, so you can't go far in life
Mental Slavery: Emancipate Yourself!
You were born a female, so you always be behind the male
Mental Slavery: Emancipate Yourself!
You don't have a Godfather who will push you to a great high
Mental Slavery: Emancipate Yourself!
You are too young to achieve great things legitimately
Mental Slavery: Emancipate Yourself!
You did not go to Ivy schools
Therefor you can't have an Ivy life.
Mental Slavery: Emancipate Yourself!
You were born into a small village
Tribe or nation and therefore you can't get to the top-most top
Mental Slavery: Emancipate Yourself!
You live in a third world country and therefore
You must carry a third-world mind you
Mental Slavery: Emancipate Yourself!
You are black
Great inventions is for other races
Mental Slavery: Emancipate Yourself!
Corruption is a game for the successful

You can't make remarkable progress without joining
The bandwagon of those that swim in it
Mental Slavery: Emancipate Yourself!
You must be terribly diabolical to make great progress in life
Mental Slavery: Emancipate Yourself!
You must belong to a Cult Cabal or Society to be known
Make progress in life, feared or celebrated
Mental Slavery: Emancipate Yourself!
You must sell your soul to the devil for your name
To ring loud in your field of endeavour
Mental Slavery: Emancipate Yourself!
You must ….

Certainly,
None but ourselves can free our minds
As a man thinketh in his heart, so is he
You have all it takes to get to the top-most top
Just emancipate yourself from mental slavery!

Works Cited

1. https://www.un.org/en/global-issues/youth

2. Edeipo Osiriame. Our Youths Have Gone Mad Too. Oasis of Greatness Publishers Limited, 2017.

3. https://www.premiumtimesng.com/news/headlines/265484-buhari-criticises-nigerian-youth-as-lazy-uneducated.html

4. 4. https://guardian.ng/news/house-of-reps-asks-government-to-declare-national-emergency-on-ritual-killings/

5. Achebe Chinua. The Trouble with Nigeria. Heinemann Educational Books, 1983, P. 16-17.

6. Al Maltoum Mohammed bin Rashid. My Vision, Challenges In The Race Of Excellence. Motivate Publishing, P. 39-40, 59, 60, 94,116, 129-130, 196.

7. Owu Festus. Laying On The Dagger's Tip. Oasis of Greatness Publishers Limited, 2019, P. 53-59.

8. https://edition.cnn.com/2015/08/03/africa/the-story-of-kunta-kinte-the-slave-who-fought-back/index.html

9. Egbuji Gloria. Election Violence In Nigeria: A New Perspective. Jesonia Communications Limited, 2019, P. 53-59.

10. Edeipo Osiriame. Sack The Wicked Chequebook Revolutionist. Oasis of Greatness Publishers Limited, P.10-11, 16-17.

Chapter Three

ANDREWS: CHECKING OUT

> *I believe that, as long as there is plenty, poverty is evil*
> *– Robert Kennedy*

Writing this book evoked a lot of childhood nostalgic feelings in me. As a child in primary school in the mid-eighties, I remember sitting in front of my Dad's Black and White Kenwood television as the golden voice of Delta State born singer, VenoMarioghae permeated the entire parlor with passion and unparalleled patriotism for her Father's Land. Permit me to reel out a portion of that most relevant song today because is the center focus of this chapter:[1]

Andrew no check out oo

"say what?"

Stay and build your country

Nigeria go survive

Na who go die for you oo

Nigeria go survive

Blood is thicker than water

Nigeria go survive

If Andrew do him work oo

Nigeria go survive

And me I do my work oo

Nigeria go survive

If our leaders do them best oo

Nigeria go survive

Andrew go stay to help oo

Nigeria go survive

..

This music legend sang this song when things in Nigeria began to go bad and Nigerian elites began to seek greener pasture outside our shores. She, however, made two striking statements I wish our then government and subsequent ones, gave or give serious considerations. She said **"If our leaders do them best oo,"** **"Andrew go stay to help oo"**. It is unfortunate that many of our leaders have not done their best or rather, their best have not been good enough. Therefore, every day by day, Andrews are checking out to our collective detriment as a nation. Let me post one sad example of "Andrews" that checked out and met their Waterloo before they got to their final destination. It was captured in Saturday Telegraph Newspaper of November 18, 2017. The article reads: Italy Hold Funeral for 26 Drowned Nigeria Women:[2]

A mass funeral was held in Salemo, Italy for 26 young Nigerian women who drowned while trying to cross the Mediterranean Sea. The simple ceremony was held in the city with 26 wooden coffins with a single white rose placed on each lid. A Roman Catholic Bishop and Muslim Imam both said prayers at the ceremony. Out of the 26 women, only two of the women were identified. Marian Shaka, who was married, and OsatoOsaro were the only two that were named. Both women were pregnant. The bodies of the 26 victims were retrieved from the Mediterranean Sea on Nov. 3 by a Spanish rescue ship. Those who died were believed to be as young as 14. 64 people are still unaccounted for and feared loss, bringing the total dead to around 90. A recent IOM report had estimated that 80 percent of Nigerian girls arriving in Italy by sea might be trafficking victims. "It is very likely that these girls were victims of trafficking for sexual exploitation" said Federico Soda, director UN migration agency IOM for the Mediterranean. IOM said at least 2,925 people died trying to cross the Mediterranean from January 1 – Nov. 5 against 4,302 last year. Libya authorities are working with the Italian government to block migrants from leaving Libya, leading to a sharp fall from the summer.

My heart was greatly touched the day I read this newspaper report and till date, I am pained to note that the terrible economic hardship in this country is forcing thousands of persons to flee our shores on a daily basis. What made marriedpregnant women to leave Nigeria through the harsh Sahara desert - possibly with the full permission of their husbands must be very grave. Don't forget that the report says persons as young as 14 years also made attempt to *"Jakpa"* as my "Lagosian" brothers will often say. If in less than 2 years, 7,227 persons died trying to cross the Mediterranean Sea and there is a huge possibility that more than

70% of all such persons are Nigerians, then it gives us an idea of how bad things have become. Many of the girls are said to be victims of trafficking for sexual exploitation but do you know that these days, some persons know *ab initio* that that was what they were going to do when they get there and they joined the train because, the hunger in their bellies have driven them to sickening height? Sir/Ma, there is terrible hunger in Nigeria and millions of people are involved! When I say millions of people, I mean literate and non-literate, young and old, male and female and will you be surprised if I should add, rich and poor? Yes some persons that appear rich – Bankers, Engineers, Doctors, Lawyers, Lecturers, etc – many of our best brains are leaving or warming up to leave and I will shortly show you the simple rational behind this preventable mass exodus. But before I do, I want to say, may God bless the Italian people and government for giving them decent burial and placing a single white Rose on each coffin. Did you know that if it were in Nigeria a mass burial like that is to take place, the person that was asked to organize the burial will most likely pocket the money of the Rose flower and get the most inferior coffin available in that locality and when he is to give invoice to the appropriate authorities, the invoice will contain all the expenses and the items will be at the rate of superb quality? If men can be callous enough to embezzle money meant for living workers and pensioners, will such a person find it difficult to siphon the money of the dead? That is a talk for another time.

Now let's go back to track. I remember a story my mum told us that is highly laughable in the present day Nigeria but was not a consideration in the late 70s and early 80s in our shore. She said my Dad, a Lieutenant in the Nigerian Army, asked her to travel to London in 1979 to give birth to my immediate younger brother and she declined. What was the singular reason? She said it was because she knew that women that newly put to bed in England were not given food that contains pepper! As a typical Yoruba woman that had four children as at that time and knows the taste of many goodies that goes with the "special pepper soup" the Yorubas make for women that newly put to bed, she was not ready to sacrifice that treat for what the British considered appropriate for women of her type. Moreover, Nigeria Military Hospitals then were at par with hospitals in Europe by all standards, so why stress herself? Today, 10 out of 10 women in Nigeria that are given that kind of offer will jump at it without giving the offer a second consideration because, to be candid, there is little or nothing to consider.

An online report says "up to the year 1985, the naira was equivalent to the Pound Sterling and stronger than the Dollars, yes Almighty Dollars[3]". Today the situation is best described as ugly, very ugly. As I write, a Dollar is being exchanged for as high as ₦585 and the Pound Sterling is exchange for between ₦700 and ₦760!

Let me do a little calculation that will make you appreciate the gravity of those figures. When the Dollar was exchanged for ₦360, it follows that someone who lives in Nigeria and save ₦100 a day will need to do so for almost a year to able to compete financially with someone that lives in the US that saves $100 in just a day of same year. Now that it is ₦585, a man or woman in Nigeria will need to work and save same amount for a year and more than six months to be able to compete financially with someone that worked and save for just one day in the US! How does that affect us as people? Pretty soon all choice properties and businesses in Nigeria will be owned by Nigerians in diaspora or complete foreigners. If foreigners come to buy up everything in Nigeria and more than 80% of Nigerians work for them, is that not a direct return to the colonial or slave trade era?

Did you know that the average factory worker's pay per hour in the United States as I write this piece is 15.41 dollars? Let us assume a hustling Nigerian works in two places and puts in 8 hours every day and works for 26 days of the month, what does that translate to in Naira?

8x15.41x26x585 = ₦1,875,088

If he spends 75% of that amount for food, accommodation, transportation and other needs and saves 25%, do you know that that is ₦468,772? How many Professors receive such amount as their gross earnings in Nigeria? Sir/Ma, the situation is ugly, very ugly. Let's compare apple with apple. What is the take home pay of a professor in Nigeria per month? Between ₦381,695 to ₦501680[5]. In the US, the monthly salary of a Full Professor is $9,926.92 and that is about ₦5,807,248 and an Assistant Professors earn an average of $4,514.42 per month and that is about ₦2,640,933![6] Can you see that the salary of a junior Professor in the US is four times bigger than the salary of a full-fledged Professor in Nigeria and the salary of a full-fledged Professor in the US, is ten times bigger than his counterpart in Nigeria? If not for patriotism, why should any Professor remain here? It's not just that the pay is poor but basic social amenities like steady power supply, good roads, pipe-borne water and so on are a mirage. ASUU strikes and all other man made bottlenecks we find in Nigeria, do make a refined academic sick every day. So to be honest, "why should Andrews not check out?" Why have our leaders not done their best?" For Nigeria to survive our leaders MUST step up the game. If minimum wage is now N30,000 and a bag of rice sells for between N25,000 and N27,000, one is forced at times to wonder how many Nigerians manage to make ends meet. I am at times more interested in the Micro Economy of our nation than our Macro Economy because the former affect virtually everybody in the nation directly than the latter. Let me cite an example of what I mean. Imagine that a young Nigerian got a job and his take home pay at the end of the month is N40,000 while he spends N12,000 for transportation. Now that in less than a year, transport fares have doubled in virtually every part of the country, he will now pay N24,000 for transportation and that leaves him with a balance of N16,000. If his boss refuses to increase his salary because he too is trying hard to keep his head afloat the murky waters of economic hardship in this country, how will the young man use N16,000 to payhouse rent, feed himself and handle other basic needs? The crazy rate of inflation of goods and services in this country should of a necessity, give our leaders sleepless nights and on a practical note do, something very fast to fix our economy. Else, more Andrews are preparing to move their bags to the ends of the earth.

Nigeria is massively blessed with all manners of resources that should make her truly great. Imagine the huge number of employment and massive wealth that will come our way if we on a serious note, begin to mine our non-oil based natural resources. We must put stringent measures that will checkmate the greedy nature of our public and government office holders and begin to reward excellence without recourse to religious or tribal sentiments. This is one of the keyway out of the mess we currently find ourselves. Flip to the next chapter to see another abnormally in 9ja my father's country, the place of my birth and the only place for now I can freely move about without fear of embarrassment from their Immigration Offices.

Works Cited

1. https://www.stelladimokokorkus.com/2019/09/music-legend-veno-marioghaes-nigeria-go.html?m=1

2. Saturday Telegraph Newspaper. Italy Hold Funeral for 26 Drowned Nigeria Women.Nov. 18, 2017. P.5

3. http://www.gamji.com/article9000/NEWS9144.htm

4. https://www.talent.com/salary?job=factory+worker

5. https://www.currentschoolnews.com/salary-structure/professors-salary-in-nigeria/

6. https://www.talent.com/salary?job=professor

Chapter Four

ANDREWS: CHECKING IN

As long as poverty, injustice and gross inequality exist in the world, none of us can truly exist – Nelson Mandela.

No man is an island neither is any nation. In modern times, most nations attain rapid growth on all side based on the number of foreign investors they are able to pull to their shore or the number of their citizens that returned home to establish flourishing business after such nationals have acquired fantastic exposure abroad. What often prompt such persons to return home is when they hear that the government of the day is friendly and to a large extent, basic social amenities like electricity, good roads, etc have been provided or are being provided. Tax holidays, attitude of government officials and the general attitudes of the country's nationals to investors and security of life and property are other determinants that woo people to a nation.

In Nigeria, the aforementioned factors are seriously lacking. I have heard of Nigerian couples that brought their children from Europe and other advanced countries to Nigeria on vacations and after the third visit of being "entertained" by the buzzing sound of mosquitoes amidst NEPA's "regular," the kids told their parents that they should never bring them to Nigeria again. Inasmuch as I don't completely agree with the children's stance, the truth that must be told is that, many things that are "normal" in Nigeria are completely "abnormal" in many other countries. One can only appreciate fully what I am saying when one travels to more advanced nations and stays there for many years. Most things done here will look very awkward when one returns to Nigeria and truly, they are.

A young Nigerian based in Sweden came to the country and he was treated in ways that made him to literally shed tears and vowed never to come to Nigeria again. A taxi driver that saw him cry asked what the matter was and decided to take him to Human Rights Radio, Abuja - where the down trodden in Nigeria go to and without any form of discrimination, get their complicated matters solved in a jiffy. He met the Ordinary President of the Extra-Ordinary People of Nigeria – Ahmed Isah and here is his narrative as can be found online.

> My name is Ndubuisi Ekulonu. I came from Sweden, I left Sweden on the 9th and got to Nigeria on the 10th. At the airport in Sweden, we were given a form from the Federal Government of Nigeria and all of us from Europe were required to fill the form. I fill mine and was given two options: Its either I pay with my card or I pay on arrival. Because of the bad network in Nigeria, I choose the option of paying on arrival so, on getting to Nnamdi Azikwe Airport Abuja here, I used my ATM card and I showed them at the airport that I have fill the form and they saw the capture and they say I should give them my passport number, I give them my passport number and they keyed it into their computer and they give me their POS that I should make payments. I

brought out my ATM card, my Zenith Bank ATM card and paid and instantly I was debited N42,750. I checked online and found out that the money has left my account. They give me two options of where to do the test. They asked me to go to either the Lab in Jabi or another in Maitama. Because I live close to Maitama, I choose the one in Maitama. But if you put the address of the Lab they gave in Maitama on Google, it will take you to one Cindy Lab in Emma Plaza. When I got there, the personnel the the Lab say they don't know anything about what I'm talking about and requested I leave their office. I was about to have a face-off with them, when the Manager of the Lab stepped in and told me its possible Google misled me. So, I came out of the place and I met a Security Man and I told him to please direct me on how to get to the place the airport officials asked me to go do the test. The man asked me to go to This Day Dome. I went there and was further directed to Ministry of Health Secretariat. When I get there, they also directed me to a place called MM - its a Conference Centre. I had no option than to go to MM and that was how I finally found the prescribed Lab. Then, I told the guy I met at the office to look at my receipt that shows evidence that I have paid them to do my Covid 19 test and get the certifications that will enable me leave Nigeria soonest and be able to catch up with work by

Monday. The guy said okay, let him forward my details to Lagos. He did and I spent the rest of the day with them without any feedback from Lagos. Till 4pm when he closed for the day, we got no response and he requested I go home. I went home but by 9am the next day, I was there when the staff resumed work. The chap checked his system and my name was not among the names he got from Lagos. While in that dilemma and fortunately for me, 2 people that boarded the same flight that brought me to Nigeria, came and they too couldn't find their names. Even my friend that came from Sweden came and he couldn't find his name. They told me if I really want to do the test, I have to pay another money. So, I paid another N42,750 to them there and they did the test.

This morning I got a rude call. I am supposed to leave Nigeria on Saturday and the caller told me that I have to go and do another test and pay another N42,750. I was in a taxi when I got the call and began to shed tears. The taxi man saw me cry and said he knows where to take me and this matter will be resolved and here I am in your midst. We were like 200+ passengers in that flight. If each of us are made to pay thrice for one test, imagine the money involved and the untold pains we were all made to go through. Honestly, if I leave Nigeria on Saturday, I won't come back.

(Please note that the narration was in pidgin English but the Author made a very close translation of his narrations to good English in order to appeal to a wider audience. Please watch the live narration on: https//youtu.be/By_TpXNoK44).

What makes a man to cry in public is often very grave and for that young man to cry and resolve not to come back to Nigeria shows the degree of resentment he now has for Nigeria and some Nigerians. It is a very bad omen for this country and it is only God that can tell how many persons have made such decisions. In the same video, a young man said he has an uncle that has dual citizenship – Nigeria and US. The said uncle has resolved never to come to Nigeria with his Nigerian Passport. Reason? He noticed that he is given better treatment when he comes to Nigeria with his American Passport than when he comes with his Nigerian Passport. In the true sense, should this be the trend? The attitude of some bad Nigerians have given us bad names internationally and therefore, many of our nationals that have integrity and are diligent are going through hard times outside there. If they manage to return home and they are treated worse than they encounter out there, don't you think that we as a nation, are forcing them to go and never return with the hard currency and vast wealth of knowledge they have acquired over there? Why should Nigeria be the place Nigerians find difficult to visit and when they do, they don't have rest of mind because of the attitude of both the government (represented by her officials) and the people themselves? When one establishes a company or send money home to set up a project and all the investments are plundered or money defrauded, should our government not put stringent measure to deal with the Nigerians responsible? I follow Senator Shehu Sani on Twitter and he once twitted about some Spanish businessmen who invested $54 million to establish a tomato factory in Kebbi State but they had to run for their lives because of the activities of bandits. Isn't that a serious setback for our country? A wise female client once advised me in my early days as a businessman, that I should always strive to give my clients the best service they deserve because a client tells 5 persons of good service rendered but tells 13 persons of bad service(s) rendered.

With the poor state of the Naira against virtually all currencies, we need to step up the game by returning to production of goods. For me, the Naira began to lose its value when many manufacturing companies left our country due to many ill factors and we did not make any attempts to call them back or change our attitudes. An enabling environment must be provided by our government that will welcome not only our Andrews that have checked out but other genuine investors in the abundant human and natural resources that abound here. Our leaders must stop paying lips service to infrastructural development and stringent measure must be set up to deal ruthlessly with erring government officials and our nationals that are giving us bad names. The attitude of our Customs, Immigration, Police and other paramilitary groups must be reviewed and made to comply with international best practices. Our Andrews that have checked out are willing to check in because of a truth, there is no place like home – if home truly has all the elements of home. Who will make Nigeria a home for all?

Work Cited
1. https//youtu.be/By_TpXNoK4

Chapter Five

THE BLOOD OF NIGERIA

*National Security' is the root password
to the Constitution
- Phil Karn.*

Blood is thicker than water is a common adage in Nigeria and it was coined not just because physically blood is denser than water but because the blood is question in the blood of human beings and human blood has physical, spiritual, psychological and emotional connotations. Blood is also very vital to man because it's virtually the only component of the man's body that interacts with all the other parts. It does not just move about aimlessly but it gives oxygen and nutrients to all the parts it gets to. The day it stops flowing is the day a man cease to exist.

A lot of factors lead to the stoppage of the human blood - sickness, accident, gunshot, machete cuts, old age, etc. None prays to die young because a lot of uncertainty lies in the world to come and those left behind will undergo untold sorrows. It is quite unfortunate to state that, the rate at which human blood is been shed in Nigeria today is terribly alarming. North – Bandits and Boko Haram, East – Unknown Gunmen, West – Ritualists, South – Kidnappers. The reasons for the killings span a wide range - money, fame, religion, ethnic differences and so on. But the actions of these killers can be best described in the song of the late Nigerian music icon, Fela Anikulapo, "they leave sorrows, tears and blood. Dem regular trade mark." When not just an individual life is threatened but a whole village or town or a vast community, then it calls for worry, serious worry.

The question any wise heart will ask is: "Where are our security operatives that get paid every month out of tax payers money when life is sniffed out of our countrymen?" "What happens to the billions of naira that is yearly allocated to defence and security matters?" "What about the numerous security votes that our top politicians get every month? Why can't they sanitize their state with it?" "Why do we mobilize tens of thousands of security personnel to monitor an elections but can't mobilize same number of security personnel to comb a forest or hide out of this persons that have vowed never to let peace reign in Nigeria? Honestly they are more questions begging for answers than the answers themselves.

No matter how small or insignificant a terrorist or terrorist group is, the best approach is to silence it before it spreads. I can liken treating terrorist groups with levity to deciding to keep a baby Python at home as a pet. One will not find it difficult to feed the beast when it is young. However, the bigger it grows, the more its appetite and the more the individual will have to labour to keep the preying eyes of the python away from him. But a day will come that the man for some reasons may not be able to act fast and the Python we have no other option than to feed on him.

Let me give a practical example of what I am talking about. Once upon a time in this country, white men were the target of kidnappers. When the company the white men work for pay ransom, he or they, would be released. After a while, many white men left and those that remained, began to go with serious security backup that will not allow anybody to think or act stupid but "the boys" appetite for "free" money has enlarged. They then began to kidnap rich fellow-Nigerians. And when our rich men stepped up their game, the boys turns to anybody they can find on the streets. Today the dimension of kidnaping across the nation is massively outrageous. Some terrorist groups don't do so on the surface for money. They could come in the name of a religion or one sentiment or the other but one thing is clear: ECONOMIC BENEFITS or, puts it in one word, GREED is ALWAYS the major brain behind most terrorist activities. Someone at the background or at the fore that have something he stand to gain immediately (or hopes to gain in the future) often triggers participation or sponsorship of terrorist activities. Every man has the right to be greedy but it is the sole responsibility of the State to checkmate it. Let me paint a picture, if a shepherd notices that a wild animal like a lion comes to his sheep pen to steal his sheep and he does nothing about it, the lion will continue to have a field day but if he builds an electric fence around the wooden pen, he will simply fold his arms and watch a good movie. The lion would either get electrocuted on its next attempt or run for its life if it manage to escape. It will then vow not to come back again. I believe that it is the responsibility of a purposeful government to provide an "electric fence" that will shield all Nigerians from all the terrorist groups that are now within our shores.

For me, all terrorist groups are worse than witches and wizard. I make such claims because I have noticed that witches and wizard are abhorred in all societies because they are known to perpetuate evil and the peak of their activities is the termination of human life through diabolical means. If we abhor those that kill through diabolical means, why should we not much more abhor those that shoot, slaughter, rape, burn or dehumanized their fellow human being? Again, I want to state that, all terrorist groups are worse than witches and wizard and it is the solemn duty of a purposeful government to checkmate them. Those that claim to fight for one religion or the other (or one ideology or the other) are not excluded because no true religion or godly pursuit prescribes all the evil we see and hear them do.

My big sister has a widow friend that lost two of her biological brothers in less than 48 hours. What happened? She got a call that one of her brothers died due to illness and she quickly called on another of her brother to rush to the village to see what to do to his remains. He got to the village and a terrorist group attacked the entire village and got the young man killed. If you were that widow how would you feel? There are a thousand and one other pathetic cases that one can readily cite but my take is: Nigerian government must begin to take drastic measures to prevent the shedding of the blood of Nigerians - both within and outside her shores. The rubbish we see and hear South Africans do to Nigerians in the name of xenophobia should be addressed with all the seriousness it entails. Great Nations of the world don't play with their citizens within and outside their shores. If we want to trend on the path of greatness, then we must drop tribal and religion sentiments when issues of preservation and protection of human lives are raised because we are all first humans, before we become tribal or religious.

I will sign off this chapter with a humorous talk that someone sent to me on WhatsApp. I wish I know who the author is, so that I can give him or her appropriate credit. The title is: Women Are Smart.

> My husband was a big drunk. Each time, I was called to pick him up in bars and terraces. Some of my family and friends wanted me to leave him but I was hopeful that I would find a solution. At one point I was so tired that I said to myself that I must find a solution very quickly. One day I went to pick him up, he was completely drunk as usual, instead of taking him home, we started heading to the morgue. I negotiated with the Mortuary Attendant to have him sleep near the corpses, then I went home. Two hours later, my dear gentleman husband wakes up and begins to beg the Mortuary Attendant that he is not

dead. The Mortuary Attendant whipped him very hard, even saying among other things: "You corpse, you come to practice witchcraft here. Go lie down with your witches and wizard friends. I've better thing to do". After pleas upon pleas, he ended up being released and he trekked home sweating profusely. Since that day, even Soda water drink, my alcohol friendly husband does not take it anymore. He is now on water only. When alcohol is advertised on TV, he changes the Channels instantly and pretend that the Station is not okay. I pretend not to notice and agree with him.

There are always "Mortuary Attendants" to cure a man's madness. Let our government rise to the occasion and think on their feet like this smart woman and with ease, terrorism will be a thing of the past in all our shore. For now, I hold my peace on this matter.

Chapter Six

KIDNAPPERS Vs MONEYNAPPERS

Corruption is a cancer, a cancer that eats away at a citizen's faith in democracy, diminishes the instinct for innovation and creativity.
— Joe Biden, President of the United States.

The word kidnappers in Yoruba Language means "Gbomogbomo" and if one translates it to Pidgin English, it will be "Carry Pikin, Carry Pikin". If we borrow a leaf from that analysis and we beam our search light on my new coined word "Moneynappers", it will mean "Gbowogbowo" in Yoruba Language and "Carry Money, Carry Money" in Pidgin English. I think this best describes the attitude of some persons in Nigeria. They keep carrying out collective money and afterwards, tens of millions of persons suffers for their misdeeds. Honestly, I can never find enough words to sympathize and empathize with the victims of kidnappers. The physical pain, emotional trauma, societal stigma, inadequate rest, etc. that they undergo are simply mind blowing.

But I want to say that the damages done to us as a people by Moneynappers are far worse than that of the kidnappers. I have watched with great amazement the speed at which some State Governors and their legislator counterparts passed bills that prescribe life imprisonment or death sentence for kidnappers. Kudos I say but … I will be happier if we make such law too for people that steal public funds. What impact do you think a law that stipulates total removal from office and imprisonment (for a minimum of 10 years with hard labour) for public or government office holders that steals between N1,000 and N10,000,0000 of public funds; life imprisonment if he/she steals between

N10,000,001 and N100,000,000 and death by hanging or electrocution for those that steal above N100,000,000? The culprit and his/her entire family are to be banned from using public facilities like government owned hospitals, schools, loan and so on. His/her spouse and their first generation children will never be allowed to hold any public office or work in any government establishment. If such laws are made and effected without fear or favour, do you think there will be sanity in all sphere of our national lives and we will begin to have tremendous progress in Nigeria our father's country? The undisputable correct answer is a Capital YES.

Thousands or millions of persons often get their hands, legs, head, in short entire body burnt due to the greed of some of our public and government office holders. The painful thing is that people that stole our money in time past are never repentant. Many of them keep looking for new avenues to steal more by contesting election into public offices or lobby "dirtyly" for Public Offices.

Another thing that baffles me about Moneynappers is the reckless way they spend money. The day I was told that there is a bottle of wine in this country that sells for ₦2,500,000, I was lost in thought for about one week, meditating about such callousness. A top government official was even fingered to be bold enough to drink four bottle of that wine in one night – that translate to ₦10,000,000! Have you ever approached a commercial bank for a ₦1,000,000 loan as a "nobody" that is just trying to build a business? By the time they gave you their criteria and ask you all manner of questions, including your great-grandmother's maiden name, you will be forced to look elsewhere. But here is somebody spending ₦10,000,000 on alcohol in a night! That is what Late Fela Anikulapo will call "Demonstration of craze, craze demonstration"

Until we de-attractivetize politics in Nigeria by making public office holders to be fully accountable for monies in their custody, to a very large degree, things will not change in this country and politics will continue to be a do or die affair.

When we de-attractivetize politics, all "professional" politicians will go get a skill, learn a trade or go back to school. We need technocrats and sound academicians to pilot our affairs if we must climb the ladder of success and command our due respect among the comity of nations.

But the million dollar question is: How do we de-attractivetize politics or the mad clamour for public offices in Nigeria? I have a little suggestion and I stand to be corrected. We use to have over Seventy Political Parties that has now been reduce to Eighteen but we have always had just two Anti-Corruption Agencies and perhaps – the Nigeria Police will make them three.

All these Anti-Corruption Agencies are to a large extent, puppets that are being controlled by the government of the day. If you are in their good book or cross over to their party, you will always be "clean" in the eyes of the public irrespective of the money you "nap". Immediately, one is in disfavor with the ruling authorities, these agencies will be released after the individual like vicious dogs that have been starved of food for many days and release to bite what is appealing to them. Each bite will be massive. But equity demands that what is good for A, should be good for B and what is bad for A, should also be bad for B.

So, I advocate a situation whereby a regulatory body will be set up to coordinate Non-Governmental Anti-Corruption Agencies. The modalities of setting them up, their framework and guidelines should be handled by forthright experts that are drawn from different fields. Rewards for exposing corrupt public and government office holders should be a major part of the package. In a country like Nigeria where more people seems to be on the queue waiting to steal than those already stealing and yet we all expect things to change, there must be practical and efficient machineries that are put in place to ensure a total collapse of this vicious chain.

The principle of **plea bargain** that many thieves of public funds often lean on to get away with their atrocities must be revisited. If a man steal ₦10,000 and is arraigned and sentenced to 3 years in prison but a man that stole ₦10,000,000,000 is made to pay ₦4,000,000 and goes home to sleep on his bed, of what use is that kind of justice? If it will warrant us to go borrow leaf from nations (like China) that are hard on stealers of public funds and adopt their template, so be it. The earlier the better because if the ever increasing pace of stealing public funds in Nigeria continues unabated, we may as well wake up to find out that someone has sold the entire nation to another country and shared the money to those he feels can talk. That may sound ridiculous but never forget that the throats of a greedy man and the grave are alike. Both are never satisfied. The only difference is one can be regulated, the other cannot.

These are my thoughts on how to checkmate stealing of public funds in Nigeria. What about yours?

Chapter Seven

NIGERIAN PRESS: PATRIOTISM OR HYPOCRISY?

> *Only a free and unrestrained press can effectively expose deception in government. And paramount among the responsibilities of a free press is the duty to prevent any part of the government from deceiving the people and sending them off to distant lands to die of foreign fevers and foreign shot and shell - Hugo L. Black.*

I was a little boy in primary school in the mid-80s when the news of a corrupt government official that embezzled large amounts of public funds and ran away to London but was almost smuggled back to Nigeria by the then Military Government of President Muhammadu Buhari filled all Media houses. What made the news weighty was the method used. He was drugged buy some Israeli contacts hired by the Nigerian government and an endotracheal tube was placed on him to prevent him from choking on his vomit while he was being transported in a crate. The operation was foiled at the last minute and it resulted to a huge diplomatic row between Nigeria and Britain for 2 years. About 10 years after I graduated from the University, the man at the centre of the diplomatic row between the two great Nations finally died. What shocked me was the several fantastic articles that many Media houses churned out concerning him. Hardly did I read any that talk about him in any bad light and I became like one of the animals at the tail end of George Owen's Animal farm. I could not distinguish the difference between the "feuding men and pigs."I had to go read about the late man again to reassure myself that I have not become too "old" as to have lost touch with my cherished childhood memories – a period the long-a-throat of many persons in this country was still at its infant stage.

Many persons in Africa, especially in Nigeria, don't like to talk about the evil committed by a man that has passed on for many reasons. But my take is: If the living knows that he will die someday, why do terrible things that will make the living to talk when he transit to the world beyond? I leave that talk for now. I have discovered that the last things many Nigeria public office holders will want to happen is negative or bad publicity. They don't mind doing bad things but they will never want anybody to talk about it. Some that are very powerful, have good rapport with virtually all the media houses in Nigeria and hardly do any negative information about them fly. Some even own Media Houses and dictate to them what they tell the public. With reckless abandon, such Media Houses (permit me to put it in pidgin English) "blow hot lies" to the public to the satisfaction or admiration of the "Oga at the top"and to the detriment of more than two hundred million people. If men are afraid to talk about their callousness, will same applies to God?

The cock is said to crow not because it has been captured. It crows because it wants the world to know that it had been captured and possibly come for it rescue. This is the primary duty of the Press. Irrespective of who is involved, the press is expected to do the noble job of informing the public the truth position of the matter without fear or inducement. I strongly believe that the degree of the active nature of a country's press, often go a long way to determine the behaviour of her public office holders. When the press begins to do their work professionally, the executive, legislature and judiciary arm of government will have no option than to sit up and effectively do what is expected of them.

The press is arguably the fourth arm of government in all democratic States and is a formidable force in all types of government. Unlike the executives, legislators and judiciaries that are directly funded by the State, the State does not directly fund Media outfits except government owned Media establishment. The press is, therefore, expected to be an unbiased watchdog of the official three arms of government. They are to report the good, the bad and the ugly side of the people in government. Doing this task without reservation has been greeted with a lot of victimisation in many societies in time past and in our present dispensation, the story has not changed. The United Nation as the universal watchdog of the excesses of individual nations, has declared May 3rd of every year to be World Press Freedom Day.[1] It is a day set aside to assess the degree of press freedom around the world, protect the press from vicious attack from any quarters and honour brave journalist that may have paid the supreme price in the line of their noble duties.

As earlier stated, no nation or individual that wants to excel in life can afford to be painted black in the eye of the public. For me, the fight to maintain a good public image is worse in Nigeria. I once interviewed a politician and off camera, he told me that "politics in Nigeria is little work and plenty noise". Anybody that lives in Nigerian knows that to a very large degree regrettably, he is right. Who can adequately help the politicians that did little work to make plenty noise? The press! This is what actually gave birth to the concept of Brown Envelope Journalism. It is a practice where journalists are settled in cash or in kind to silence the negative story or writing a good story out of an ugly one. This kind of journalism makes corrupt government and public officers holders to have a field day. As a one-time freelance journalist for over half a decade, I know what I am talking about and if you want to know more, please just Google Brown Envelope Journalism in Nigeria and you will have more than enough to read. To practically show how far the press has "derailed" from the track in Nigeria, permit me to post part of the interview that *Premium Times*' Mudiaga Affe had with a veteran journalist called Okharedia Ihimekpen. The interview is titled: How "Brown Envelope" Ruined Nigeria Journalism.[2]

PREMIUM TIMES: How would you describe the practice of journalism in your time and now?

Okharedia Ihimekpen: I entered this precarious business of journalism in the early 70s. In our hey days of yore, things were not as bad as it is now. Although it was rough then, we now have what we call digital journalism.

In those days, when you are going for an assignment, you will need a photojournalist, a car and a driver. So, you go as a crew, but today just one person can go for an assignment and he does the job of a crew with the help of your smartphone. You can even start sending your stories while the event is ongoing. There is a paradigm shift because this was not what was obtainable in those days. So, it now depends on how people can cope because the world is not static, it is dynamic. Since society is always changing, we have to change with it and that is the only way you can survive it.

PT: Has this paradigm shift also affected the ethics of journalism?

Ihimekpen: Yes, it has. These days when journalists go for assignments, they wait for brown envelopes. We did not grow up that way. The brown envelope syndrome came in at about the late 80s and early 90s. When I started practising journalism, we did not seek brown envelopes. We practically begged people for news. You are paid when you write an article for a newspaper and that encourages you to write more. You put in the effort to get news and you must have the nose for news.But these days, apart from a few dedicated journalists, the majority stay in one place and when they cover an assignment, they expect something. I am not saying there (wasn't) then, but it was not like this. Journalists of then were like scavengers, people hardly liked them, but they were feared. Journalism will not make you rich but it will open doors for you. When you walk into a gathering and introduce yourself as a journalist, they will immediately change the topic of discussion and sometimes walk away from you because they do not like you. The journalists, too, were not interested in good stories because they believed negative news was the story. That was the period we just came out from the nationalist struggle by Obafemi Awolowo, Nnamdi Azikiwe, and Peter Enahoro, popularly known as Peter Pan. We felt then that the only way we could make our name is to write stinkers. We were used to 'write and kill.'Most times then, ours was to investigate the dirty side of government or big individuals in the society. You look for a loose end and when you can unravel something new, you are a hero. I recall one of our correspondents in Rivers State went to cover Diete Spiff's birthday but came out with a negative story on Mr Spiff's wife. They (Spiff's family) were annoyed with the story so they got the reporter, beat him, and used a broken bottle to shave his hair and that instantly became the real news all over. The story became too hot that the then Head of State, Yakubu Gowon, had to intervene and they paid heavy compensation. They paid us (Nigerian Observer) huge compensations. But these days, when you talk, your colleagues will want to blackmail you.

PT: But we later shifted from 'publish and be damned' to developmental journalism. At what point did this happen?

Ihimekpen: That should be in the early 80s. We felt we cannot remain the same way forever. We started seeing it from the angle of partnership and also protecting our lives. It was at that point too that the military started giving some carrots. When some journalists started getting these carrots, we felt we could improve ourselves. So, people like Peter Pan, who was my mentor, whom I described as someone who has written so much on earth and torn the sky with his pen…. he was the Editor-in-Chief of the old Daily Times at the age of 21.Although the military was throwing the carrot, they were also very hard and when you are caught, they will be hard with you.

PT: How did brown envelopes become a common feature in journalism?

Ihimekpen: It was the encroachment of the military ideology, military mentality, like that of the former military president, Ibrahim Babangida, for instance, who was so strong that he was able to 'oligopolise' all the institutions in the economy.

When there is negative news, he felt he could buy his way through. In the early 80s, I was with the Esama of Benin, Gabriel Igbinedion, in one of his business conglomerates, Okada Air. They brought some aircraft and one of his sons organised a ceremony to launch the new fleet. He proposed that money should be given to journalists who came to cover the event, but I told him that it was not necessary. I told him to wait and appreciate whoever does any good report. He rebuked me and went to report me to his father. The father told me that I wanted to destroy his business, he told his son to give money to the journalists. I told him that I would not be part of what they planned to do.

The event came and they shared the money with journalists. One small newspaper in Lagos called *Lagos News* and *New Nigeria*, who did not get from the largesse went to do their write up. They described the new fleets in Okada Airline as refurbished aircraft. You know the negative news is the main news and their report overcrowded other news reports. The then Minister of Aviation, Jeremiah Useni, had to query the airline over the refurbished aircraft. They (management of Okada Air) started running helter-skelter and their father (the Esama of Benin) realised the usefulness of my advice and called me to come and establish *The Speaker,* a newspaper. So, you will find out that the brown envelope was good and bad. If well managed, it could be good for you but when badly managed, it could be bad.

PT: Would you say the gratifications that journalists receive today in the form of brown envelopes is good?

Ihimekpen: No, it is not because it has turned journalism into ridicule. For instance, I will not encourage someone to become a journalist now because it will not make you rich. Brown envelopes have become what some journalists survive on. It is an unfortunate situation and one of the publishers of a leading newspaper in Nigeria (name withheld) once told me that he does not need to pay journalists that he employed because he believes that his company's identity card has given you the window to make money. This is someone who read English from the University of Benin and was groomed in the Nigerian Observer. The brown envelope has helped to reduce, diminish, and denounce journalism, and sometimes you are not treated softly and nobody takes you seriously anymore. It has also made a few good journalists lazy because they have become copy and paste specialists. People will go for an assignment and only one person will write the story and they make the mistake of sending the story to their head office with that person's by-line. There is also the political aspect of it by the Nigeria Union of Journalists (NUJ) who admits all sorts of persons because of elections.

PT: In your heydays, you found your way into the sickbed of the late Ambrose Alli, a former governor of defunct Bendel State at the University College Hospital (UCH) in Ibadan, despite serious military protection. How were you able to do that?

Ihimekpen: That period, I was still writing for the Nigerian Observer in Benin City. When he was arrested and being tried during the era of Muhammadu Buhari, we felt it was a case of natural injustice. His offence was that he signed on his complimentary card and that was when people became wary of writing at the back of the complementary cards. The late governor, Ambrose Alli, wrote something at the back of his complimentary card and gave it to Gabriel Enaboefo, the then Director of Organisation of the defunct Unity Party of Nigeria (UPN) in the state. The card permitted him to collect a particular sum of money from a contractor for the party. It was less than N1 million. After using it to collect the money, Mr Enaboefo retrieved the complimentary card and kept it. So, when he was arrested during the military era, to defend himself, Mr Enaboefo presented the complimentary card as his defence that he did not steal any money. It was that money that was used to rope Ambrose Alli in that matter and his security votes. The former governor tried to defend himself but they did not listen to him but eventually, he was sentenced.

Same with the late Bola Ige and other civilian governors in the botched Second Republic. Initially, we were seeing Mr Alli during their trial in Lagos, but suddenly we were no longer allowed to see him. They brought Mr Alli, the late Abubakar Rimi, Alex Ekweme, and others to Agodi Prisons and Mr Alli fell ill in the prison and was brought to UCH.

Some of us, including Omo Ikhiroda, Sam Iredia, and I would go to UCH to try to see Mr Alli, we would not be able to see him. We learnt his health had deteriorated. Mobile police and soldiers were always guarding his hospital room. After some time, we started monitoring the movements of all the personnel around the hospital, including the security people and we found a loophole. We took advantage of it.

I mastered how to use the camera and after one week of

practice, I got dressed in a medical doctor's robe and went into Mr Alli's room. Mr Alli was shocked to see me because he was not expecting anyone at that time, I told him to be calm, and he recognised me.

I took several pictures of him and asked a few questions, he responded. He was very apprehensive. I took five different shots and left. I met the soldiers outside drinking and cracking jokes. We left for Lagos immediately. We gave the pictures to Tribune and some other media. By the next day, it was a front-page story, "Alli on the line, counting hours." Other newspapers copied it. By the third day, there was a riot in Ekpoma as students started criticizing the state Mr Alli was in. The military authorities tried to find out who the reporter was. They saw that it was not fiction and that Mr Alli even talked to me. We were declared wanted by the military. But the whole idea paid off because they changed all the security men and they set up a committee which recommended that Mr Alli should pay back some money and be set free. The same leverage was extended to Bola Ige and others. It was the Esama of Benin, Gabriel Igbinedion, who eventually offset the money for

Professor Ambrose Alli, through some arrangements. That was how Mr Alli was let off the hook.

PT: Do you think journalists of today in Nigeria can take that kind of risk?

Ihimekpen: No, they are not daring. Although there is still some form of investigative journalism, those that will put the life of the journalist at stake is no longer done. The wife or husband of the journalist will even query him/her.

PT: How can we change the face of journalism?

Ihimekpen: Unfortunately, journalism has become a dumping ground for graduates. In those days before you are employed as a journalist, you write feature stories which they use to judge those who are qualified to practice. The use of English, syntax, and presentation, among others. But now these are not there today. The field has become one for all comers. So, I think the situation should be reversed.

Honestly, from the narratives of this interview, one can clearly see that a lot has gone wrong with journalism in Nigeria. Integrity and professionalism which ought to be the watch word of media personnel have been relegated to the back ground in many circles. Persons that everybody know as dubious or outright thieves now cheaply get good publicity as long as they are willing to part with good Naira notes. These days, we find two or three Media Houses covering the same event but there is great disparity in their reports. Little investigation will show clearly that "Brown Envelope" made the pen of some of them to write what never happened or made the fellow to "play the tune" of the "piper." If the likes of Pa. Okharedia did not risk his life to do is work without expecting a handsome gratification, Late Prof. Ambrose Alli might have as well died in prison without the record being put straight.

But do we still have some bold and selflessness men in the media space of Nigeria? My answer is a capital yes! Ordinary President, Ahmed Isah of the *Berekete Family* stands tall in this regard. His Human Right Radio and TV Station in Abuja has put handsome smiles on the faces of tens of thousands of persons across all the states of Nigeria. More grease to his elbow. What about Mr. Efe of *Man Around Town* and his crew in Independent Radio, Benin City, Edo State? Their candid views on many issues has given credibility to journalism in no mean degree and made a lot of government and public office holders to sit up. Mr. Oga Tom Uhia of *Power Steering Magazine* is another dogged publisher that has been in and out of police cell for his fearless report of sensitive news. Mr Eric Osagie, Publisher of *THIS NIGERIA* is another veteran media personality that I respect a lot for his forthright stand on reporting issues the way they are. Dapo Olorunyomi (the recipient of 2020 International Press Freedom Award and a co-founder of *Premium Times*) and Musikilu Mojeed (the recipient of the Wole Soyinka Investigating Reporting Awards and The Editor-in-Chief of *Premium Times*) are two solid media Irokos that I ceaselessly admire from a distant. Peter Emuekpere, Publisher of *Development Monitor* and his "Guided Missile" column is worthy of mention among the media giants in Nigeria.I doff my media hat for great columnist like Abimbola Adelakun of *The Punch*, Olukorede Yishau of *The Nation* and Owei Lakemfa of *The Vanguard.* Their pen has consistently refused to call black white. I just wish they keep it up. Last but definitely not the least, I will make mention of Olusegun Adeniyi, the current Chair of the Editorial board of *ThisDay Newspaper.* His pen gore oxen without fearing its owner(s). Thumbs up sir.

There are many others that want off space or my limited knowledge will not allow me to acknowledge but one thing is sure: God and posterity will DEFINITELY REWARD EVERYONE according to our works on Earth. For me, it is far better to do a good job and have little publicity than do a bad job and get good publicity. What do you think? If the press is pressed, what is the Hope of Nigeria?

Works Cited

1. https://www.un.org/en/observances/press-freedom-day
2. https://www.premiumtimesng.com/news/headlines/428166-interview-how-brown-envelope-ruined-nigerian-journalism-ihimekpen.html

Chapter Eight

THE WAY OUT OF A SINKING SHIP

A nation is alive only when it grows,
constantly discarding its outdated traditions,
habits, rituals and assumptions
- Abhijit Naskar.

The defunct Bank PHB once ran an advert on all available means of media of that era. The advert read: *One day cars will run on water. Need financing to buy the Atlantic?* The advert made a lot of sense to me because my knowledge as a mechanical engineer tells me that the final product of perfect combustion of petrol is mainly water. And when water undergo electrolysis, hydrogen is separated from oxygen and hydrogen standing alone can produce great energy. To make it commercially viable is what the world is yet to discover and that bank did peep into the future to predict its eventual possibility.

The future we talked about a decade ago is perhaps, the today we currently find ourselves. The rate at which knowledge increases these days is so alarming that failure to update one's knowledge yearly might make one to be primitive in his/her approach to issues, and that, within a short pace of time. To embrace the future and be an active player in it, one must be willing to learn and re-learn at all times. This is the key to a glorious tomorrow.

The kernel of this chapter is crude oil, her children and the role they play in our national life. It is an open secret that Nigeria does not just depend on crude oil for her survival but she is heavily dependent on it. A source said oil account for 40 percent of our GDP, 70 percent of our budget revenues and 95 percent of foreign exchange earnings[1].

If up to 95% of our foreign exchange is derived from crude oil and anything happens to crude oil, what will happen to our country? For me, we have depended on oil for too long and it is unfortunate that many still don't see that the glorious days of petroleum product are fast fading off. Crude oil is like a ship that is gradually sinking and the situation demands urgent action if chances of survival is to be a possibility.

I began to fear for the future of this country, fourteen years ago when Barrack Obama was elected the 44th President of the United State of America and the first black man ever to occupy the White House. Like all black men, all over the world, I was excited and joined his inaugural ceremony from one corner of Nigeria. I listened with rapt attention to his speech for a while and my joy soft pedaled when I heard him say the following:[2]

> We'll restore science to its rightful place, and wield technology's wonders to raise health care's quality and lower its cost. We will harness the sun and the winds and the soil to fuel our cars and run our factories. And we will transform our schools and colleges and universities to meet the demands of a new age. All this we can do. All this we will do.

When "the sun, wind and soil" are harnessed to "run cars and factories", what becomes of crude oil that occupy more than 90% of our foreign exchange? That was when I had expected our leaders to swing into action and begin on a very practical note to diversify our economy or means of generating foreign exchange.

The closest I have seen any Nigerian leader do in this direction is the pet project of the former governor of Delta State, Dr. Uduaghan. It was tagged: Delta Without Oil. Was it truly executed and followed up? If yes, what are the dividend and if not, why?

Dubai is where she is today because of this proactive nature of her leaders. Let me quote again from the book of my wonderful friend from a distance – Mohammed bin Rashid Al Maktoum - *My vision, challenges in the race for excellence*

> Rising demand for aluminum for example, drove the Dubai Aluminum Company (DUBAL) to raise its production to more than 151,000 tonnes by 1983. The proceeds of exporting this amount of aluminum stood at AED 460 million (US$125 million) and represented about half of Dubai's non-oil exports at the time. Ever since, DUBAL has kept expanding its production capacities, reaching 722,000 tonnes in 2005 - Pg. 89

> Our economy is nevertheless growing continuously, because we have succeeded in boistering the non-oil sectors and developing new industries, which generate US$37 billion (AED 136 billion) in 2005 and

represented some 94 percent of our GDP – Pg. 91.

Dubai and Nigeria had some similarity in times past. From the above statements, both countries enjoyed the oil boom of the eighties but where they differ from us is that when they were enjoying the dividend of oil, they did not stop building other sources of their income. I believe that DUBAL is our equivalent of Ajaokuta Steel Company and Delta Steel Company. In the eighties, these companies were fantastic and gave the Nigerian government serious revenue. I wish I have statistics to prove my point as my friend did in his book. We allowed those companies to die and the billions of Naira or Dollars that we spent to set them up, all went down the drain. Just imagine that as far back as 2005, oil gave Dubai (a country massively blessed with oil) only 6% of her revenue, while non-oil sector gave them 94%. That is super fantastic and their leaders deserve a standing ovation for that. With the uncertain nature of Crude Oil in the International Market and the rapid/continuous search for alternative power sources that is currently going on in the world now, I am certain that oil, most likely by now, gives Dubai less than the aforementioned 6%. The nasty blow COVID-19 lockdown gave to the world economy (especially Crude oil sales), ought to have taught us a huge lesson but instead of diversifying with the little we have, all I hear is "Let's borrow." Borrow to do what? How many factories have we built with the money that was borrowed or how many moribund companies like Ajaokuta Steel Company have revitalized?

Honestly, our leaders need to wake up. Our over dependence on sales of crude oil have made our leaders not to think of how to make many other resources that is country is blessed with viable. In my previous book *To Serve Nigeria Is Not By Force,* I dedicated Chapter One to the great exploits of ancient and modern Nigerians and the vast Natural Resources God scattered all over this blessed country. We have one of the best weather in the world; more than 70% of our land are agriculturally viable; we have large deposit of minerals in all the States of Nigeria and honestly, we have hyper intelligent people in this country that can technically and managerially handle any establishment to world class standard. This is a huge possibility when we tackle greed – a small portion of corruption that has seriously dealt with us as individuals and as a nation. What has happened to groundnut, cocoa and palm oil that were our major source of national revenue before crude oil displaced them? Do they still have great market value till date? The answer is a capital Yes! Then why did we stop their production in commercial volume? The answer is very simple. Majority of our leaders are always waiting for monthly allocation – in simple term "money from the proceeds of crude oil". This trend must cease. Each governor should be made to develop the resources in his State and make remittance of an agreed percentage to the National. I mean rather than wait for allocation from the Federal Government, they should develop and manage the resources in their domain as Businessmen and not Supervisors or "Executive Governors". This is the summary of Resources Control that many persons have been yearning for and I think this is the best time to implement it before things finally get out of hand. Is there a possibility of that? Yes! When most countries that currently buy crude oil from us stop buying because Obama and Bank PHB's prophesy has finally come to pass, we will then be forced to think otherwise but that may be too late to jump out of this sinking ship. I see a progressive Nigeria that is not dependent on crude oil or any single stream of income emerging very soon. As I sign out of this chapter, please permit me to post one of my poems that perfectly handles my aforementioned position. It is titled "I hail my Igbo brothers[3]". Enjoy:

1. HAIL MY IGBO BROTHERS

I hail my Igbo Brothers
Wonderful brothers of the Lolo 1 of my dynasty
My best friend and one who washed my kids' infant heads

I hail my Igbo Brothers,
Men who felt 9ja's economic pulse and therefore gave soothing
names to the love of their lives

Oriaku they gave
When 9ja was gay
Meaning one who has come to eat wealth.
Odoziaku they gave when 9ja slid
And it means one who helps to manage wealth
*Akanakpata-aku*they gave
When 9ja's economy fell apart and our bellies cried aloud
And it means the hands that helps to build wealth

I hail not our some of political class
Who live in the past
Who greedily eat what is left when they should build from
there
I hail not some of our Executive
Who execute our purse
Eating and eating when they should be building and building

I hail not some of our Lawmakers
Who make fat purse for themselves
And the more they take, the less we see

I hail not some of our Judiciary
Who for a tip, take a leap
While our purse is pilfered to naught

Wake up, Your Excellency!
The days are gone when all you do is eat and eat.
Wake up, Your Excellency!
For we no longer need eaters or managers but **STRICTLY BUILDERS**.

Wake up, Your Excellency!
This time, you MUST fold your sleeve and work
Hard and hard, until the purse is filled
Wake up, Your Excellency!
Oil Boom is now a mirage
But 9ja is blessed with thousands of others that can make her
BOOM again

If you wake up
I will have no choice than to hail you
As I have hailed my Igbo Brothers
Nigeria Kwenu! Iyaa!

Works Cited

1. https://openknowledge.worldbank.org/handle/10986/18078
2.https://www.theguardian.com/world/2009/jan/20/barack-obama-inauguration-address
3. Al Maltoum Mohammed bin Rashid. My Vision, Challenges In The Race Of Excellence. Motivate Publishing, P.89, 91.
4. Edeipo Osiriame. Sack The Wicked Chequebook Revolutionist. Oasis of Greatness Publishers Limited, P.

Chapter Nine

BUY MADE IN NIGERIA

*Patriotism consists not in waving the flag,
but in striving that our country shall be righteous
as well as strong
- James Bryce.*

To say that Nigeria is blessed with diverse natural resources is a truth that only an ignorant person will argue. A foreigner once visited Nigeria and he kept shouting "look at money! Money everywhere" The Nigerians he was talking to felt he was beside himself but I tell you the truth, he was far from being insane. Most expensive and ornamental items like gold, diamond, jasper and so on are never attractive in their raw state. It takes a man who truly knows their worth to go looking for them in very remote places of the world. He then passes the raw materials through some refining process and finally, polishing. When it is finally place on a very beautiful case and taken to Five Star places of the earth, the value of that "undesirable" but now transformed object become so massive that at time, millions of dollars must exchange hands for the owner to let it go.

The day this truth sinks into our minds as citizens of this great nation, our nationals will no longer export her numerous raw materials to other nations of the earth because when they transform these raw materials from us and bring them back as finished goods, we often pay through our nose to get them. Why can't we be the ones doing the transformation to finished products? That is the first challenge I want us as a people to give serious considerations to.

Secondly, when we have some persons that decide to convert our raw materials to finished products, many of our nationals look down on the finished product and prefer to buy the ones form other shores. This mindset has done us massive harm than good. Some years back, anything that is fake was said to be from China.

Today, nobody dares say so because they have so developed their skills that there is no quality they can't readily give you. How does this talk concern Nigeria you may ask?

Please let's read this headline article of *The Guardian Newspaper* of January 14, 2021 that was written by Fred Adekoya and Saxone Akhaine. It is titled: Why Textile Sector Remains Brink Despite Interventions[1]:

> Despite years of intervention, Nigeria's textile industry is a departure from the ideal, owing to challenges of huge appetite for importation, poor patronage, policy implementation and a broken value-chain. According to stakeholders, if only 10 per cent of the yearly import bill of $4 billion textile fabrics is re-invested into the textile industry, the country would be a net exporter and expand its revenue from programmes like the African Growth and Opportunity Act (AGOA) of the United States. Stakeholders say the problem of the industry transcends funding, because interventions so far, have helped to increase capacity to access raw materials like cotton and retooled machinery, but poor patronage draws back the gains.

> Cotton grows in 26 of Nigeria's 36 states and West Africa is the fifth-largest producing region globally. With CBN's intervention, operators noted that Nigeria now produces excess cotton but lacks an industry and market regulation that will uptake the raw materials for production. Exporting raw cotton creates further

problems for the industry as value-added products continue to dominate importation.

Industry data showed that in 2019, 18.6 per cent of all imported cotton worldwide ended up in China, the largest exporter of textiles and clothing products in the world. Chinese imports currently account for 60 per cent of the print fabric market in Africa, with India supplying an additional 21 per cent. West Africa itself is a large market for prints and buys around 65 per cent of all foreign imports. Nigerian demand accounts for around 38 per cent of total imports in the region. Specifically, they noted that the Executive Order 003 of 2017 signed by President MuhammaduBuhari has remained active on paper as Ministries, Departments and Agencies (MDAs) of government still import their uniforms from abroad despite local capacity for such apparels.

Similarly, the procurement of school uniforms from abroad by many private schools and rising dependence on used clothing and apparel by many Nigerians continue to undermine the growth of the textile sector. For African prints like Ankara, operators noted that distributors have broken the value-chain and now import directly from China with made-in-Nigeria labels.

Data from the National Bureau of Statistics confirmed that Nigeria's importation of textile materials has been on the rise, with the country recording N200.6 billion worth of goods as at Q3 2020. The country exported N5.05 billion worth of goods during the same period.

Last month, the manufacturing PMI for the textile, apparel, leather & footwear sub-sector remained stationary, as against the recovery in November. The Central Bank had last October, said it provided cotton producers with more than $300 million in loans in recent years to support the domestic textile industry, once Africa's largest.

From about 600,000 local farmers across the country that grew and supplied cotton to the Cotton, Textile, and Garment (CTG) industries, today's reality showed that less than 25 of the over 300 textile companies that were scattered across the country are still in operation, performing below capacity, as the country depends heavily on importation. Despite the ban on imported finished textiles to protect local manufacturers and designers, having cost the economy at least $4 billion yearly, smuggled goods continue to make inroads into the country through the Benin Republic, Chad and Niger borders.... In a chat with The Guardian, the Director-General, Nigerian Textile Manufacturers Association (NTMA), HammaKwajaffa, explained that a large percentage of textiles sold in the country are smuggled and imported, putting the country at a loss in potential yearly Value Added Tax (VAT) revenue from such activities. He added that if the 10 per cent levy from textile importation was properly invested in the sector, it would have grown and developed capacity to tackle competition.

He identified the suspended payment of Export Expansion Grant (EEG) claims as adding to the woes of operators, thus limiting their capacity to export and even improve production, since the markets have been dominated by foreign clothing. According to him, operators have been selling below production costs and this has remained unsustainable, noting that five of the 25 remaining firms are into fabrics while the others are in the allied sector. "Our numbers are being decimated daily. Distributors no longer buy from manufacturers but go to China to import. This is a country that used to have 867 textile mills in the 80s. Today, we have excess raw materials but low capacity to uptake for production as the market depends on foreign goods. "The executive order 003 is inefficient. No one is complying with the law. No one is addressing the decayed infrastructure and overhead costs. Energy costs are also huge and affecting operations of manufacturers. The textile development levy has also not been diverted to the sector for growth. The levies are supposed to be used to support the industry rather than seeking loans. We are running only one shift rather than three shifts and this has also affected capacity utilisation cum employment," he lamented. He also traced the origin of the problems to 1995 when Nigeria replaced the Multi-fibre Agreement (MFA) with the World Trade Organisation's (WTO) Agreement on Textiles and Clothing (ATC).

With the replacement, Nigeria had to remove all protection of its local textile industry, rather than securing special arrangements with the WTO, such that the local textile industries would be protected until they were independent.

According to him, the WTO agreement opened the Nigerian market to cheaper textile imports, predominantly from China, as well as second-hand clothing from the United States and Europe. However, before the expiration of the MFA, the United States had introduced the African Growth and Opportunity Act (AGOA), an initiative that opened up the American market to African countries to export to the U.S., but instead of African countries enjoying the window opened to them, China with its textiles proved stronger and took over the U.S. market.

Some of the stakeholders disclosed that Nigerians and not Chinese are to be blamed for the sector's woes because it is Nigerian businessmen that usually take the samples of local fabrics to China to reproduce.

MEANWHILE, officials of the National Union of the Textiles and Garment Union of Nigeria (NUTGWN) have blamed collapse of the Industry on non-implementation of policies initiated by the Federal Government to salvage the ailing sector. The President of NUTGWN, John Adaji lamented that the few surviving textile factories that are producing less than 50 per cent of installed capacity are downsizing as a result of redundancy. Adaji, who spoke with The Guardian on the poor state of the textile industry, said government did not take advantage of the existing huge to address the problem of unemployment and youth restiveness. He blamed government for non-implementation of the Cotton, Textiles and Garment (CTG) policy, which it initiated, to the letter, particularly the Executive Order 003, meant to ensure that Nigerians patronise made-in Nigeria fabrics. He said full implementation of that Order would have boosted the manufacturing activities of the existing factories and pave way for revival of the industry. He said: "They came out with an Executive Order, called 003. It was meant to address the problem of patronage. Which means that all government parastatals would be encouraged to patronized locally produced goods. That is what the executive order is meant to address. And if that has been taken seriously, the story today would have been different for us in the textile sector. "Like we always say that the leadership is supposed to lead by example. So, if they see these policies as problem solving, you then start the implementation from the top.

Direct the Federal Executive members, even if it is once in a week or twice in a week to ensure that what they wear is made-in-Nigeria. There should be a legislation to back it up." "The legislators will also obey the Order. Then you see, the chunk of it all is through the implementation by the Nigerian Army, Police, Air force, Navy and other paramilitary forces. We also have customs, immigration, federal road safety commission, civil defence, unity school, and NYSC. The uniforms of all these organizations are enough to provide 50 per cent boost and market to the local producers in Nigeria, but the Government has refused to implement the Order. "This is the miracle of South Africa. And it should be imbibed here in Nigeria. We borrow policies from other countries, but we don't have the political will to do the same thing here. This, I tell you will produce 50,000 direct jobs into the sector. So, the executive order is meant to address it."

As usual, let's analyse this article together:

Executive Order 003 was signed by no other but Mr. President but the report say it "has remained active on paper". Did you know that for you to import anything that is manufactured in China to China, you will pay import duties that will hardly allow you to sell the imported goods, let alone make a profit? From this article, it is very glaring that both government agencies and our individual businessmen are culprits in this crime against our economy.

Despite the ban on imported finished textile products, large volumes of finished textile still end up in our country. Who is to blame? What is the statutory duty of Custom Personnel? What massive efforts have we made to beef up security not only in our usual boarders but in all the perimeter of our national boundaries?

When these items finally get here, why do Nigerians prefer them to the ones here? In as much as I don't support mediocrity, the need to build our local industries must be the priority of all – especially our leaders. When you say I should buy made in Nigeria goods but I look at you and you are wearing foreign shoes and your wife's attire from head to toe are all foreign, why should I not take your talk with a pinch of salt? When you ban importation of rice and foreign wine but when I go to State functions I am served foreign rice and forcign wine, will I not understand your hypocrisy with ease? If we have one or two persons in Nigeria that manufacture cars in Nigeria and they are not massively patronized so that they can create more employment and improve the skills of our youths, how do you expect such persons to improve his brand and be a world player?

It is shocking to note that less than 25 out of over 300 textile companies that use to be in Nigeria are now left. This fact is indeed very ridiculous because it has a terrible chain effect. As the number of companies in our shore decreases, the unemployment rate in our shores automatically increases, the value of our naira depreciates and our dependence on imported goods will increase. Never you think or talk about foreign goods without you thinking or talking about the foreign currency that must exchange hands.

When you always got to them, the value of your money is bound to depreciate. Decrease of companies in this country is also a sign that the purchasing power of the nation is on the decrease because no factory works in isolation. There are many small and medium scale businessmen that must render service to these companies that will make them live comfortable lives and pay taxes comfortably. We have many things to lose any time a company folds up or relocates to another country.

65% of all textile imported to Africa, comes to West Africa and Nigeria takes 38% of the entire figure. Is it surprising? With a population of more than 200 million, we have a huge market that is very attractive to any serious minded businessman. If we make a policy that states that once we have any item that we can meet its production locally 40 – 50%, we will be truly block our borders to its importation, you will be surprised at the rate at which many companies around the world will rush to set up their branches in Nigeria. We must begin to plan and act this way.

Why should the uniform of our Military, Paramilitary and NYSC not be completely manufactured in Nigeria? One may argued, "The Nigeria materials is inferior". My reply is simple. What quality did the person that placed the order make with the company? To maximize profits, many will deliberately ask the company to produce poor quality. "After all, it is government thing. The people must use it" many greedy contractors will say.. No Sir! No Ma! The era of this kind of mentality must be eradicated. Do you know that the reason many prefer to buy foreign good is because it will be difficult to detect their fraudulent practices? The report says if all these agency begin to truly buy their uniforms from local manufacturers, it will boost their production by 50 percent and do you know what that means? Many persons will be employed to meet the demand and our GDP will, increase. If 50,000 direct jobs will be created, then more than 500,000 indirect jobs will be generated. So, what is stopping it from happening?

For things manufactured in Nigeria to gain the recognition and patronage they deserve, the following steps must be taken:

"Excellence" or "quality" must be the major interest of the manufacturer because fake or substandard product, spoils business anywhere in the world.

Sentiments of every kind must be dropped. Why refuse to buy a product from a fellow Nigerian because he is not your tribe but you go outside the country to buy (over there). Is that person over there from your tribe?

There must be a conscious effort to shield our local producers/manufacturers from their counterparts (out there) that are stronger than them. The cost of production of a company that produces 100 million of a product can never be the same with a company that can only produce 50,000 copies of the product within the same time frame.

Executive order 003 of 2017 is fantastic. It must not be allowed to remain on the papers where it was written. All hands must be on deck to make it work.

Nigeria's excess raw materials must no longer be allowed to waste or lie fallow. Both government and the private sector must bring in all the necessary machines to convert them from raw materials into finished products. A possibility? A capital Yes.

I see a glorious Nigeria when we produce and consume 60% to 80% of what we need locally. What do you see?

Watch out for my next book that is titled "I Pledge to Nigeria, My Country".

Works Cited
1. Adekoya Fred and Saxone Akhaine. Why Textile Sector Remains Brink Despite Interventions. The Guardian Newspaper, Jan. 14, 2021. P. 1-2.